I

ICONS OF SOCIAL CHANGE

Scharada Bail is a writer, internet consultant and Tarot practitioner. She has won several writing awards and her books for children include the travelogues *Footloose on the West Coast*, *Malwa on My Mind* and *A Necessary Journey*. Scharada lives in Chennai with her family.

ICONS
OF
SOCIAL CHANGE

Scharada Bail

Portraits by
Sujata Bansal

PUFFIN BOOKS

PUFFIN
Published by the Penguin Group
Penguin Books India Pvt Ltd, 11 Community Centre, Panchsheel Park, New
Delhi 110 017, India
Penguin Group (USA) Inc., 375 Hudson Street, New York, New York 10014,
USA
Penguin Group (Canada), 10 Alcorn Avenue, Toronto, Ontario, Canada
M4V 3B2 (a division of Pearson Penguin Canada Inc.)
Penguin Books Ltd, 80 Strand, London WC2R 0RL, England
Penguin Ireland, 25 St Stephen's Green, Dublin 2, Ireland (a division of
Penguin Books Ltd)
Penguin Group (Australia), 250 Camberwell Road, Camberwell, Victoria
3124, Australia (a division of Pearson Australia Group Pty Ltd)
Penguin Group (NZ), cnr Airborne and Rosedale Roads, Albany, Auckland
1310, New Zealand (a division of Pearson New Zealand Ltd)
Penguin Group (South Africa) (Pty) Ltd, 24 Sturdee Avenue, Rosebank,
Johannesburg 2196, South Africa

Penguin Books Ltd, Registered Offices: 80 Strand, London WC2R 0RL, England

First published in Puffin by Penguin Books India 2004

Text copyright © Scharada Bail 2004

Illustrations copyright © Sujata Bansal 2004

Typeset in Palatino by Eleven Arts, Delhi-35

Printed at Pauls Press, New Delhi

To

All the architects of social change in this book,
the hundreds of others engaged in the process,
the many who have died resisting powerful, armed and
exploitative forces

and

the memory of Mahatma Gandhi – supremely inspiring
Karmayogi

CONTENTS

ACKNOWLEDGEMENTS

I would like to thank the following people and organizations for their help in researching and writing this book:

Aruna Roy, Sugatha Kumari and Rajendra Singh, for sparing the time to talk to me.

India Together <www.indiatogether.org>, for permission to use material from Sandeep Pandey's speech.

Rediff.com <www.rediff.com>, for permission to use material on Ela Bhatt and Aruna Roy.

Humanscape <www.humanscape.com>, for permission to use material on Aruna Roy.

World Press Review <www.worldpress.org>, for permission to quote from Deepak Mahaan's interview of Aruna Roy.

Seagull Books, for permission to quote extracts from *Dust on the Road: The Activist Writings of Mahasweta Devi* edited by Maitreya Ghatak.

The Ramon Magsaysay website <www.rmaf.org> and the Samachar website <www.samachar.com> were very useful references.

In addition, the websites I found useful were:
<www.sewa.org>
<www.sulabhinternational.org>
<www.ashanet.org>
<www.soscvindia.org>
<www.bengalonthenet.com>
<www.literateworld.com>
<www.indiainfo.com>

The award-winning Marathi book *Johad* by Surekha Shaha, available to me as a Hindi translation by Bal Urdhvareshe (*Sumeru*, 2003), was a very valuable reference for Rajendra Singh and the Tarun Bharat Sangh (TBS).

I am grateful to all the individuals and institutions who made this material available, and am solely responsible for any shortcomings in my own accounts of the 'Icons'.

I would also like to thank Sayoni Basu of Penguin Books for being so supportive of this book from the concept stage to the actual execution, and Sudeshna Shome Ghosh for her copy-editing.

PREFACE

As children in today's developed and connected world, you are well aware of the seductive power of oft-repeated messages.

We live in a world where our attention is claimed every moment by what is attractive, pleasing, useful and marketable. Advertisements ask us to buy those goods and services that are supposedly brighter than the brightest, and better than the best. The news that we see and hear highlights the achievements of people who supposedly have wealth, fame and success. If we are to be taken in by the make-believe world so successfully created, we would imagine that detergents could wash away all human dirt, and ice-cream could take away all hunger!

But even in the relative comfort of our lives, glimpses exist of how grim and difficult life can be for others just like us. Problems of poverty and deprivation, of the social, economic, political and physical handicaps that people suffer from, make every day a grim struggle for many, where surviving with dignity seems almost impossible.

Many of us choose to simply block this out. Life is difficult enough for me, we say. But there are some men and women who possess the courage and the conscience that cannot stay still in the face of another person's suffering.

This book is about the men and women who have chosen to tread on the difficult path of creating social change, of bringing about changes in the hearts and minds of men and women, so that people can live with more dignity, more ease. These men and women are not often seen on our TV screens. But their work, their courage, and their humanity make them greater heroes than others who have received more tangible rewards. Together, the people in this book have helped make India a better place for millions of our fellow citizens. Individually, each has a story of struggle, sacrifice, setbacks and eventual victory that should be an inspiration to all of us.

I hope that you will enjoy these stories of contemporary social activists as much as I have enjoyed writing them. I felt I knew my country and its people a lot better after writing this book, and I hope you will feel the same after reading it.

MAHASWETA DEVI

THERE IS A DRAWING ROOM in Kolkata, visited every day by scores of visitors. Men and women, both young and old, and occasionally children have made their way to this room which is liberally endowed with books and papers. Here they are received by a lady whom they familiarly address as 'Ma' or 'Didi' or 'Marang Dai' (meaning elder sister in Santhali).

They sit before this woman of deceptive frailty, who is in her seventies. She notes down their stories as they talk to her. Tribal people from Purulia, or Medinipur, or even as far away as Palamau in Bihar, relate their personal stories to their 'Ma' in the total confidence that she will do everything in her power to help them. Whether it is a child who has been kidnapped, lack of drinking water, fears of attack by other groups in their village, or police atrocities, these people are not afraid of placing everything before this woman. They know that she will write letters on their behalf, or phone high officials and more humble ones, or anything else it takes to get justice for her tribal friends.

'So what about the village representatives of the Samiti (Paschim Banga Kheria Sabar Kalyan Samiti)?' asks the woman, at some stage of the narrative of a man and his teenaged son.

'They accompanied us to the police station, but the new inspector did not listen to them or us. This boy has spent fifteen days in the lock-up for no crime! Now the employment exchange officials say he cannot get a job because he has a criminal record!' The father is speaking with some emotion, but his son sits quietly, observing the woman's total attention in recording every detail. 'If anyone can help us, it is this determined woman,' he thinks. He has heard many stories among his tribal peers of how Didi has the power to pick up the phone and move the most inert official machinery to redress some wrong.

Mahasweta Devi, the frail-looking woman whom the tribals turn to for help, is one of the most distinguished writers and activists in India. Among the many awards she has received are the Sahitya Akademi Award in 1979, the Padma Shri in 1986, and the Jnanpith Award and Ramon Magsaysay Award in 1996. While many of the honours have been for her writing, an equal number have been for her fearless campaigning for some of the poorest and most neglected people in Indian society.

Born on 14 January 1926 in Dhaka, Mahasweta Devi was educated at Rajshahi and later at Vishva Bharati, the famous university set up by Rabindranath Tagore in Shantiniketan. It was from Vishva Bharati that she passed her Intermediate examination in 1944, and later started her career as a school teacher in 1948. After getting her Master's degree in English in 1963, Mahasweta Devi began teaching as a lecturer in Bijoygar College in Kolkata, where she taught until 1984. By then, her reputation as a literary giant and a vocal social activist had become well established in the whole country and overseas.

Mahasweta Devi was born into a family endowed with artistic ability and fired by social commitment. Her father, Manish Ghatak, was a writer and poet, and her mother Dharitri Devi was a social worker. The famous film director Ritwik Ghatak is her uncle—her father's younger brother. She married Bijan Bhattacharya, a founding member of the Indian People's Theatre Association (IPTA) who was well known as a playwright and actor. Her husband encouraged her to take up writing. Mahasweta Devi's first book was published when she was thirty.

It was a biography of the spirited queen of Jhansi, Laxmibai, a woman who had led her people to fight the British army in the First War for Independence in 1857. *Jhansir Rani* was no ordinary biography. Mahasweta Devi used myths, legends and ballads about the Rani of Jhansi to add many layers to her narrative. Before she started the work on the book in 1954, she decided that she needed to get to the place where the roots of her subject lay. Therefore she left her home in Bengal to spend time amidst the people of Bundelkhand, whose ancestors had been the warriors in Rani Laxmibai's army.

Such a journey represented no little sacrifice on Mahasweta Devi's part. She was unemployed at this time, and her husband was also without a job. Friends and well-wishers collected Rs 400 for the journey and her time in Bundelkhand. She had to leave her six-year-old son at home. However, the choice of subject was indeed fitting—and the personal harships in pursuit of a goal was a pattern which would be repeated over and over again in her life. In subsequent years, Mahasweta Devi was to prove how courageous and spirited was her own resistance to injustice, oppression and violence. No wonder she chose Rani Laxmibai as her first heroine.

In the forty-year period from 1956 to 1996, she had written ninety-four works of fiction. Her heroes and heroines are nearly always leaders of people's struggles against exploitation—such as Birsa Munda, the tribal leader in *Aranyer Adhikar*, or Titu Mir, the peasant leader who led a revolt against the British in Bengal in 1830–31. In perhaps her most famous work, *Hajar Churashir Ma*, her heroine is not a leader, but the book examines the popular resistance to oppression from a different angle: the mother of a young Naxalite boy muses on the social and political factors that have driven her son towards an extreme position.

What makes Mahasweta Devi's work unique among her contemporaries is the manner in which she enriches her writing with many different kinds of language and speech. Her writing contains literary, bookish Bengali as much as it does the more common language of the people on the street. It uses rural idioms and city flourishes. For this, she has received much critical acclaim. But she is impatient with much of it. In a recent interview, she refused to be drawn into a discussion of language, style and creativity. 'Life is larger than any single creative work. Understand life, work to make life better. Be engaged in the struggle for life—creativity will improve by itself,' she said.

Mahasweta Devi's novels and stories are deeply rooted in her own experiences with the people about whom she writes. She calls the time spent with her subjects 'preparation' for writing. From 1963 to 1975, she went to the Singhbhum, Ranchi, Palamau and Chaibasa areas of Jharkhand every year to spend time with tribal people, who lived lives of extreme deprivation as bonded labourers and nomadic groups. They had no access to education or health facilities and were living off the meagre resources of steadily shrinking forests. Mahasweta Devi soon became involved in a movement to better their conditions. One means she has used with great effectiveness has been her literary work. Her writing reflects her deep familarity with the Santhal, Kheria and Lodha tribes. From her many stories and novels, as well as articles, essays and reports, we learn how difficult it is for tribal people to gain the facilities and privileges taken for granted in mainstream society.

Some of the tribes she has written about are still struggling to overcome the stigma of being branded 'criminals' under the British administration. Even though they had been removed from this 'criminal' status after India became independent, the local administration and the villagers around them still treated them with suspicion. Young men from these tribes are rounded up by the police for any crime committed in their locality, on mere suspicion. Through her writing, and her direct involvement with their organizations, many of which she has founded with others, Mahasweta Devi challenges the way educated urban people look at tribals and their way of life.

The development process in modern India after Independence has brought many gains for people living in cities, but the cost of this development is paid by the poor and marginalized people, who are still denied even the basic necessities. When their homes are uprooted for steel plants, mines, dams or electricity projects, tribal people rarely receive due compensation from the government in a way that allows them to rebuild their lives. Mostly, they are forced to migrate to the cities to work as casual labourers. Cities are difficult places for simple tribal people, and many employers are willing to exploit them. Many migrants fall into debt, or become bonded labourers. Those who choose not to migrate to cities have to turn nomadic and search for forest cover to carry on their traditional occupations. This brings them into conflict with landowners, the police and forest officials. Many feel hunted and victimized in their own country.

The realization of their sorry state left Mahasweta Devi deeply disillusioned. 'I was twenty-one in 1947. With many others, I tried to believe that India's independence would not totally fail the poor of the country, she writes in 'Samitis: Change Through Participation'. 'In 1984 I can say that for the poor of India, national independence, with its many plans, programmes, projects and acts in Parliament, have come to nothing. The question is, have we reached a point of no return, or is there any hope?

'I have also found that the poor of India may be mostly illiterate but they are no fools. Perhaps now they realize that keeping them in eternal poverty is very much a part of the design. People's poverty is the basis on which projects can be made, plans sanctioned, pundits enter as consultants and money inflow be guaranteed, all with an eye to see that nothing reaches the target beneficiary. They tell me so in their language, which is often unsavoury but true.'

Mahasweta Devi strongly believes that organized group action by the people left out of the 'development' process is the only way for them to get what is due to them as citizens of this country. This belief has led her to found several organizations, and she is actively associated with several others. The Paschim Banga Munda Tribal Samaj Sugar Ganthra, the Paschim Banga Bhumij Tribal Samajkalyan Samiti, the Paschim Banga Harijan Kalyan Samiti, the Palamau Zilla Bandhua Samiti and the Berhampur Municipal Sweeper Association are some of them. Her involvement with these groups, and the issues they face, is intense.

Mahasweta Devi's powerful fiction and non-fiction writing has helped many issues come into public view. She has illustrated how bonded labour can crush the lives and spirits of large groups of people. This form of labour is seen in many parts of India, but Mahasweta Devi has illustrated it most poignantly through the bonded labourers of Palamau. Bonded labour arises when poor tribals or villagers take a loan from moneylenders. The interest charged on this loan is so exorbitant that the poor find it difficult to repay the money. They are then made to pledge their services till the money has been paid back. But the salary paid to them is so meagre, that it ensures that they will never get out of debt, and never be free to go and work anywhere else.

Bonded labour also masquerades under other names. The relentless cycle of exploitation extends to the field of contract labour such as that found in the brick-kiln industry. Rural women are recruited to work on contract, miles away from their homes, and paid very low wages. Their distance from family and lack of security makes them extremely vulnerable. 'In politically conscious West Bengal these *rejas* (brick-kiln contract workers) are denied a minimum wage, medical facilities, maternity leave or any kind of leave, and, of course, the right to form a union. There is no attendance or pay register, identity card or employment card. The set-up is very cruel and very cunning,' writes Mahasweta Devi in her essay 'Contract Labour or Bonded Labour?'

Landownership and employment of tribal and rural people have a direct bearing on the lives of millions in our country. Mahasweta Devi has highlighted the problem of unemployment among tribal youth who, after completing their education and being registered in employment exchanges, wait in vain for years for the call from potential employers.

How rural workers in cement mines get affected by asbestosis and silicosis, and how eucalyptus plantations affect the underground water table are environmental themes that Mahasweta Devi has made millions of readers think about. The superstition, casteism and communalism that have rural people in their grip have been examined in her articles, and the need to combat these attitudes with education, people's initiatives and laws has been underlined. She has written with great depth and understanding about how women bear the brunt of poverty and discrimination, and how they have to rear children in the most difficult circumstances.

Mahasweta Devi's writing on social themes is different from that of others because she weaves the people's own voices, their songs, stories and speech into facts that she has meticulously researched through personal contact with them. Thus, she quotes the song a brick-kiln worker sings to her baby in the midst of her article on contract labour. She also reproduces bald official records that tell a shocking story of neglect, or worse, persecution of the poor and powerless.

The death of Chuni Kotal, a bright young woman who was the first graduate from the primitive Lodha-Savara and Kheria-Savara tribes of West Bengal, in 1992, shocked many. Mahasweta Devi wrote about this remarkable woman who had battled insurmountable odds—she came from one of the tribes notified as 'criminal' by the British—to educate herself. When the prejudices, hostility and cynicism of the academic community got too much for her, Chuni Kotal committed suicide. The entire West Bengal media pointed out that the circumstances leading to the suicide needed to be probed, and the deliberate persecution of tribals needed to be corrected.

Writes Mahasweta Devi in her essay 'The Story of Chuni Kotal', 'See the face of West Bengal, now that Chuni has ripped off the mask? A judicial inquiry? Surely not. We know that judicial inquiries in West Bengal get lost in a desert of inertia. I think all democratic organizations and people should protest against this naked caste and class oppression and demand a

CBI inquiry. Is not Chuni's death a pointer to the tribal in India? Well, Bengal has shown its true face.'

Bortika was a quarterly literary journal edited by Mahasweta Devi's father, which she took over after his death in 1979. Since then, she has transformed it into a journal where agricultural labourers, small peasants, factory workers and rickshaw pullers can write about their lives and the problems they face. From being a niche, high-brow periodical, *Bortika* has become a strong forum for alternative literature in Bengali, with many dedicated readers, even though it cannot draw the money and advertising of today's mass-circulation magazines.

Her passionate espousal of causes related to the poorest in our society, and her belief in people's movements being the path to social justice, have often brought Mahasweta Devi in conflict with governments and official machinery. In recent times, she was deeply disturbed by the communal killings in Gujarat. At the time, she had urged the then president of India, K.R. Narayanan to intervene, and put a stop to the communal frenzy, and ensure that the relief camps were kept functioning as long as there was a need for them. Typically, what upset her most was the mindset that had led to the days and weeks of violence. It is a mindset that seeks to validate communalism and casteism, and Mahasweta Devi clearly sees changing this way of thinking as a very important task for all Indians today.

In her home state too, she has often been at odds with the government's view of things. But officers in many government departments, including the district administration and the police, have a deep and abiding respect for her and her work. It is because of the respect she commands that she is often able to intervene in a personal capacity on behalf of a poor tribal from Purulia, a rural Baul singer or an agricultural worker. Just as she does not hesitate to lift her pen to write incisively on burning issues and prick the collective conscience, she does not hesitate to write letters on behalf of all these people to the concerned officials.

Mahasweta Devi's advice to young writers has always been, 'Go amongst the people, collect the facts of their lives, analyse them, write, and struggle to better circumstances.' For her, the pen has never been an ornament indicative of a writer's exalted mind. It has always been a flaming sword, poised to challenge darkness and untruth, and defend those who have no voice. Not surprisingly, millions of poor, displaced and powerless people in India hold their Didi close to their hearts.

BABA AMTE

MURLIDHAR DEVIDAS AMTE, BETTER KNOWN as 'Baba' since that was his mother's childhood name for him, was hurrying home one rainy night after finishing work. The monsoon rain beat strongly down upon him, soaking the lower half of his body, despite the umbrella he carried. There were few people about in Warora, a small town in Maharashtra, at that time of night, and Baba would have been home too if his work had not involved night labour.

Murlidhar Amte was the chairman of the municipal council of Warora. In the 1940s, while World War II was ravaging many Western countries, India was struggling against the British, and the many forms of injustice and inequality in its own society. In Warora, like other small towns, the dirt from homes and public lavatories, including human excreta, was collected by scavengers who gathered it from the drains and carried it away in baskets. The men and women who performed this job were treated as 'untouchables' by their fellow townspeople, and their wages were meagre.

When Baba Amte had taken over the municipal council as its chairman, he had organized a union for the scavengers, so that they could collectively represent their interests. But when the union asked him for an increase in salary, he turned them down, citing the lack of funds in the municipal council as the reason. 'You say this because you don't know what it is like to do this work,' said the scavengers. 'Think of how we clean latrines in the rainy season,' they added.

'Is this a challenge?' asked Baba. 'Are you saying that I cannot do the work you do?'

'Yes, we are,' they answered.

Baba Amte had never refused to rise to a challenge in all his life. He prided himself on being absolutely unafraid of anything in the world. He accepted the scavengers' challenge. 'All right, assign me some latrines. I will do your work and see for myself whether a raise in your salary is justified, even though the municipality has no money,' said Baba.

Forty latrines were assigned to him, and every evening, Murlidhar Devidas Amte joined other scavengers in cleaning the dirt and human waste in Warora. This monsoon night, he was returning after completing his scavenging duties.

As he hurried home, he noticed that on one side of the road, exposed to the rain, lay a huddled shape. As Baba came close to it, he saw to his surprise that it was a human being. He stopped, and looking down at the mutilated body of a leper clothed in rags, recoiled in horror. The features on this unfortunate man's face had long since been wiped away by the disease. His fingers and toes had melted away, turning his arms and legs into stumps, and maggots had invaded his body. Baba was completely horrified by the sight. Even his daily contact with dirt and human waste had not prepared him for this. He found some thatch nearby, and placing it over the man as a shelter against the rain, turned and hurried away as fast as he could.

He returned the next day and constructed a small hut for the leper whose name was Tulshiram. He fed him, and the man lived his remaining days being cared for by Baba.

The fear and horror Baba had felt that rainy night haunted him for months. Long after the scavengers had received their pay rise and he had withdrawn from scavenging duties, he continued to be tormented by the thought that he had felt afraid at the sight of another human being.

Leprosy was not uncommon then in the country. Its horrific

effects robbed those suffering from this disease of limbs and dignity. They often had to live out the rest of their lives as beggars and outcasts. After his encounter with Tulshiram, Baba could not erase the sight of that ravaged body from his mind. Baba's life took a fresh direction. He decided he could only conquer the fear he had felt that night by working to save and heal others like Tulshiram. About that decision, he later said, 'I took up leprosy work not to help anyone, but to overcome that fear in my life. That it worked for others was a by-product.'

This 'by-product' has benefitted thousands of people in his remarkable lifetime, and Baba's courage and selfless service have become shining examples not only to other Indians, but to all of humanity.

Baba Amte was born on 26 December 1914, the eldest child of Laxmibai and Devidas Amte, a district administration and revenue official under the British, in Hinganghat, a small town in Maharashtra. His father was a cultured and soft-spoken man, always careful and conscientious. His mother, though illiterate, was given to acts of great kindness. She would interact freely with servants and others lower down the social scale from the Amtes. This led to differences of opinion with her husband. Laxmibai's emotional nature also led to her undergoing occasional bouts of insanity, during which only Baba, the most beloved of her eight children, could communicate with her. She was undoubtedly a very important influence on him.

As a child, Baba was much moved by the plight of an old blind beggar one Diwali. The man's misery seemed in stark contrast to his own happy and comfortable life. In his teens, when he travelled with his father to the forests, he encountered the Madia Gonds, the tribal people who dwelt there. Baba loved their innocence and zest for life. He felt saddened by the extreme poverty in which they lived, eating roots and berries, with no access to education and health services. Their plight remained ingrained in his mind and later he returned to help these people, bringing hope into their lives.

From a very young age, Baba's favourite form of rebellion was to associate with the poor, neglected and outcast. He would bring the servants' children to the family dining table, and mingle with the so-called 'untouchables' without caring about the disapproval and censure this brought him from others. He was educated at home, and at the Christian Mission School in Nagpur. Although he wanted to be a doctor, his father was keen that he become a lawyer, since an astrological forecast had been made about the suitability of this profession. Accordingly, Baba was admitted to Nagpur University to pursue legal studies, and a house was set up for him in the city, where he lived in the care of several servants.

Thus began a period in which Baba tested the limits of youthful rebellion and lavish luxury. He also experienced some significant changes that would set the path for his adult life.

Baba was so well off that he drove to college in a two-seater sports car, with white mud guards and leopard-skin seats. When he went to the movies, which was very often, he bought three tickets for himself—so he could put his feet up on the two seats in front! He wrote articles for the film magazine *Picturegoer*, and fan letters to Hollywood actresses Norma Shearer and Greta Garbo, and even received replies from them.

In the midst of these heady diversions, however, he retained his affection for others less fortunate than him, and his desire to be of help. In 1935, as a student, he decided to travel to Quetta (now in Pakistan), where an earthquake had caused much devastation, to help in the relief work. During the train journey, he saved a young couple from being crushed by a large tin trunk that would have fallen on their sleeping forms. Baba rushed and caught the trunk, but shattered his arm and shoulder in the incident. Back at home, some people felt that the limb should be amputated, but Baba refused all treatment except those of a local bone-setter's, and his shoulder healed. However, it continued to give him occasional pain for many years.

He had many heroes, but nearly all of them were unusual ones. He looked up to Jesus as a hero, a wonderful human being to be emulated, not as a god to be worshipped. He learnt lessons in bravery from a thug or *goonda*, whose story created a sensation in those days. This criminal, seeing a group of men attempting to molest a girl, challenged them with the words, 'What are you doing to my sister?' He then fought singlehandedly with the group, and died of stab wounds sustained in the fight. Baba was much struck by this and later said he drew a lot of inspiration from the courage and honour of this man. He also greatly admired the Maharashtrian social reformer Sane Guruji. It was through Sane Guruji's efforts that so-called 'untouchables' gained entry into the temple of Vitthal at Pandharpur, an important pilgrim town.

While Baba was still a student, he took a three-month break in Shantiniketan, the idyllic university set up by Rabindranath Tagore in Bengal. This was a very significant period for Baba, when he could indulge his natural love for poetry, and imbibe Tagore's philosophy, which stressed living in harmony with nature. He also felt connected and closer to god, though Baba never practised any form of conventional worship after this.

In 1936, he obtained his law degree from Nagpur, and initially began practising in Durg. By 1941, he moved to Warora, where his family owned lots of land. He began to manage these estates along with his work as a lawyer. It was here that he became chairman of the municipal council. In 1942, he fought many cases for freedom fighters who had been prosecuted by the British during the Quit India movement. In secret, he supplied help, including arms and ammunition to underground freedom fighters for many years.

As World War II raged, Baba was feeling more and more dissatisfied with his duties as a lawyer and landlord. He was tired of living a life that seemed to be the opposite of his own ideals and feelings. He began to rebel against his own status and prestige. He grew a beard and walked about barefoot— completely unheard of for a lawyer. He ate publicly with Harijans, upsetting his upper-caste peers and contemporaries. He started living in a hut near a Muslim cemetery, far removed from his family estates. At this time, people began calling him the 'mad son of a mad mother'. Many years later, acknowledging how much his mother's personality had helped to make him what he became, Baba wrote an essay called 'The Madness of My Mother'.

By 1946, Baba Amte was thirty-two years old and still single. He had such unconventional ways that people doubted if he would ever marry and settle down. Then a distant relative died, leaving six unmarried daughters, and Baba helped in finding grooms for some of the girls. It was while he was attending the wedding of one of the elder girls that he noticed her younger sister Indu slip away from the festivities to help an old servant put clothes on the washing line. This glimpse was enough to convince Baba that he had found a true companion. As he said later, 'I felt married at that moment.'

Baba had to convince Indu Ghuleshastri's mother that he was a suitable husband for her daughter. He somehow succeeded, and Indu, too, accepted him. Their wedding was conducted shortly thereafter, with bride and groom presenting a weird and wonderful picture. Indu was small, petite and pretty, and a very bright student. Baba was twelve years her senior— a bridegroom with a long beard, and plastered with bandages! These he had acquired some days before their wedding, when he had encountered some British soldiers molesting an Indian girl. In the manner of the thug he admired, he had rushed to rescue the girl, and been bruised and battered in the fight.

Baba renamed Indu as Sadhana, which means hard work put in towards a goal, usually a spiritual one. After a brief honeymoon in Goa, he took his bride to live on the edge of the Muslim cemetery where he lived with his poor and disadvantaged friends. They called this community the Shrama Ashram, and the *shrama*, or labour, they did helped the whole group make ends meet. They grew and sold vegetables for a while, but adopted a unique method of selling, where the customers were allowed to set the price of what they bought. Baba noticed that the richer the customers, the less they were willing to pay, while the poor offered more fair rates! This hard-working commune had to close after an especially vicious outbreak of malaria. From the luxury of her parental home, Sadhana plunged straight into the simplicity and toil of her role as Baba's companion.

Their son, Vikas, was born in 1947, and another son, Prakash, in 1948. After his encounter with Tulshiram, and his decision to work with leprosy patients, Baba worked in a leprosy colony run by Manohar Diwan at Dattapur near Wardha for six months. He underwent this training on the advice of Vinoba Bhave, and during this period, learnt to dress leprosy wounds, feed and care for patients, remove bones and limbs affected by the disease, and administer drugs.

In 1949, Baba joined the Calcutta School of Tropical Medicine to learn more about leprosy treatment. Only doctors were normally admitted to this course, but Baba's work had already attracted sufficient interest, and Prime Minister Nehru interceded with the institute authorities to let Baba join this course. Although Baba had now learnt much to equip him to deal with leprosy patients, the conviction was growing in him that medical treatment of the disease was only half the battle. Repairing their ravaged lives, and building their confidence and trust in the human race was an equally important task. What these men and women needed was love, respect, support and acceptance, which was often denied to them by their friends, family and society at large. They were shunned by everyone after the symptoms of the disease appeared.

Baba decided that a completely different approach was needed to bring these men and women back into active life. By the time he completed his course from Kolkata, diamino-diphenyl-sulphone, a cure for leprosy had been discovered. Armed with this, Baba began to put into practice his vision, by building a self-sufficient colony which would be managed by patients. In 1949, he registered the Maharogi Sewa Samiti, an organization dedicated to helping and rehabilitating leprosy patients, with the motto 'Charity destroys, Work builds'.

The first settlers in Baba's colony were his family, six leprosy patients, and a lame cow. They moved to a twenty-hectare plot leased to them by the government. The plot was hard and rocky, with a little scrub forest cover. Life began in a thatched hut without walls, and Sadhana struggled to keep house in an area infested with scorpions and snakes, where leopards and tigers roamed at night. The first few days were extremely difficult—a well had to be dug with hand-held implements. But the leprosy patients were willing workers, and Baba and Sadhana did not spare any effort on their part. In two years' time, with some help from a pair of bullocks that Baba had borrowed from his father's estates for a plough, they had achieved self-sufficiency in growing their own food.

Baba named his colony Anandwan, or forest of happiness, and it lived up to its name. By the third year, sixty leprosy patients had made it their home. The Amte family worked and lived here, and Vikas and Prakash grew up there. But the nearby villagers still stayed away from the inmates. In 1953, a group of foreign volunteers, who had been staying at Mahatma Gandhi's Sevagram Ashram, arrived at Anandwan. They were so inspired by the place that they decided to stay and help build medical facilities. As they toiled to construct a hospital, a big change came over both Anandwan and the community that surrounded it. The Anandwan settlers were happy that they had received help, support and respect from those who considered them their equals. The nearby villagers were ashamed to think that foreign visitors could mingle freely with the leprosy patients, while they had kept away from them. Soon, they too began to interact with the Anandwan community, and a major hurdle was crossed.

Since then, there has been no looking back for this magical oasis created by Baba Amte. Today, Anandwan is a self-sufficient township with hospitals, banks, post offices, schools and colleges. It has a community centre for senior citizens, vocational training in metal, woodworking, spinning, weaving, printing and handicrafts. Its water is supplied from four man-made lakes, and produce grown on its lands is sold to nearby towns and villages.

In Anandwan, there is a school for blind children, known as the Prakashachi Shala or the school of light, where all the teachers and students are blind. There are primary schools for children with special needs, and orphans and the elderly are assigned special roles in the community so that they feel completely at home. The leprosy patients who first began living in Anandwan and who were cured could go on to live in Somnath, another community created by Baba with Vinoba Bhave's help in 1967. Many programmes to guide and aid the youth are conducted at Somnath. Ashokvan is another inspired and motivated community created by Baba on the outskirts of Nagpur. All these places give shelter, support and self-respect to thousands of differently abled people.

Baba Amte's health has suffered for many years with an illness that is affecting his spine. This form of cervical and lumbar spondylosis makes it impossible for him to sit. He can only lie down, or stand. Yet, the fire burns brightly within him to work for those whom he feels need care and attention. In 1973, he began work among the Madia Gond tribals, for whom he had felt much affection in his childhood. Their extreme malnutrition, illiteracy and lack of medical facilities needed to be tackled immediately, he felt. Thus began the Hemalkasa Project in 1975, with a fifty-bed hospital being set up in the Madia Gond territory. This is managed by Dr Prakash Amte, Baba's son, and his daughter-in-law, Dr Mandakini Amte. A school for tribal children was also started in 1974. Baba's other son, Vikas Amte, lives and works in Anandwan.

The loss of tribal homes due to forest areas being submerged by the construction of the Sardar Sarovar Dam led to Baba Amte becoming involved with the Narmada Bachao Andolan. In fact, for several years, he moved to a village called Kasrawad on the banks of the Narmada, in Madhya Pradesh. Here, Baba lived in a house called Nijibal, or one's own strength. Today, Baba Amte and Sadhanatai live a life of contentment and contemplation, with rich memories of lives spent in service to humanity.

While they have worked so hard to cure patients stricken with leprosy, the struggle to change attitudes has been harder. As Baba describes it, '. . . in so-called healthy society, you can see a lot of injustice and poverty, yet you are not moved. You have lost your sensation, your feeling. You suffer from psychological anesthesia. The mind is so dull; the heart so unfeeling, thick-skinned like a hippopotamus. That's mental leprosy. I have found out that while physical leprosy is perfectly curable, mental leprosy is not' (www.rmaf.org.ph).

Baba had taken the first steps towards his life's work as an antidote to fear—the fear he had felt at seeing Tulshiram. As he describes it, 'Where there is fear, there is no love. Where there is no love, there is no God.' It is love that destroys fear, hatred and suspicion of others. Baba is not a religious person, but he has shown us that this love is no less powerful than god. With his life and his work, he shakes us out of our unresponsive attitude to poverty and suffering. He reminds us that to be human we need to do more than just exist.

CHANDI PRASAD BHATT

THE BUS TRAVELLING THROUGH THE Garhwal Himalayas held passengers and pilgrims, local hill-dwellers and visitors from the plains. The cold afternoon air still held some trace of the rains that had recently fallen. As the driver turned a bend in the mountainous road, all the passengers gasped. Ahead of them was a sight that signalled a familiar calamity of the mountains—boulders, loose earth and the exposed roots of trees spoke of a landslide. By the time the bus stopped, its passengers had noticed a group of people gazing into the steep gorge below, down the side of the mountain road.

'A bus has been swept off the road by the landslide!' the onlookers told the passengers of the bus that had stopped.

'It is more than 300 feet to the valley below!' said another onlooker. 'No chance of any of them surviving such a fall.'

Even while the bus passengers and the bystanders discussed the accident and its possible consequences among themselves, one slim and wiry passenger had been purposefully removing his bulky outer clothes. Stripped to his light undergarments, he stood on the edge of the steep drop for a few seconds, judging the distance to the upturned bus. Then, he began making his way carefully to the bottom.

'What are you doing?' chorused the onlookers. 'They will all be dead anyway, why risk your own life?' they wanted to know.

But the man paid scant attention to their questions. As the afternoon wore on, another bus arrived, and its driver followed the example of the slim youth, climbing down the mountain slope. By the time it was evening, and the rescue team arrived, the two men had managed to bring eight wounded passengers from the fallen bus back on to the main road. Even though twenty-four persons had perished in the accident, just two daring men were enough to help the wounded eight out of the mangled bus. The courage of the young man was inspiring.

This was on 21 July 1961. After he had finished his rescue mission and dressed himself again, the young man sat and watched the scene before him, with a cup of hot tea held in work-calloused hands. The raw face of the mountain exposed by the landslide made him feel as if his own body had been hurt. The shocked and bleeding faces of the people he had rescued haunted him.

How had his beloved mountains turned so hostile? What selfish deeds of man had made the Himalayas, traditionally believed to be the abode of the gods, agents of destruction? He knew then that he had to work as hard as he could to preserve these mountains and the people they had always nurtured and blessed.

Ganga Ram Bhatt of Gopeshwar was a farmer and priest at two of Garhwal Himalaya's holiest shrines—Gopeshwar and Rudranath. When a son was born to him and his wife Maheshi Devi Thapliyal on 23 June 1934, he named the child Chandi Prasad, or gift of goddess Chandi. It was through intense prayer to the goddess that he and his wife had been blessed with their son. But he hardly got much time to spend with this child, as he died within a year of Chandi Prasad's birth. His wife, two children and widowed sister were left with no means of support.

Like other immensely hard-working women of the hills, Chandi Prasad's mother also worked on their small, two-acre plot to grow food for the family, apart from tending to their few cows, fetching water from a river some miles distant, and looking after her two small children. In spite of all this hard labour, money was in short supply, and her bright son had to drop out of primary school at the end of Class II. She could not afford to spare even the one-anna or six-paise-a-month tuition fee to pay for his education. Instead of attending school, Chandi Prasad began to attend Sanskrit classes and learn the performance of religious rituals, qualifying as a 'pandit' five years later. He now had some earnings from religious functions, and could therefore enter school again in Class VII.

At that time, Gopeshwar had facilities for studying only up to Class IX. On completing this, Chandi Prasad was sent to live and study in Rudraprayag, where he lived with a cousin whose father paid his fees. The cousin resented Chandi Prasad's presence, and his treatment of the young boy was bad enough to make him begin living in a room with fellow students in the village instead. He was determined to somehow stay in school long enough to pass his Intermediate examination, but more complications were to follow.

At home with his mother for the holidays, while attempting to lighten her burden of work, Chandi Prasad fell ill with malaria. His anxious mother treated him with traditional herbal medicines, but his strength took some time to return, and he was weak and emaciated for several months. When he recovered, it was too late to go back to school, so he decided to study for the Intermediate examination privately. Village elders convinced his mother to get him married, and he tied the knot somewhat reluctantly, with Deveshwari Dimari, daughter of a wealthy Brahmin from Chamoli.

Now began a stint when Chandi Prasad Bhatt worked as a booking clerk for a local bus company. The work was not inspiring. He attempted to leave it once and work as a schoolteacher for some months but the higher salary the bus company paid was welcome and necessary to meet his family's needs. His posting was quite far from Gopeshwar, at the end of the bus company's route, close to the hill shrine of Badrinath. It was thus that he often came in contact with Sarvodaya workers—dedicated men and women who had plunged into active social work under the leadership of Mahatma Gandhi.

In 1957, Jayaprakash Narayan addressed a public meeting at Pipal Koti, the small town where Chandi Prasad worked. This meeting was organized by Mansingh Rawat, a gifted and illustrious young man who had turned away from a promising academic career to do community work. Rawat wanted to spread the ideals of the Sarvodaya movement among his own people in the hills. The meeting, Rawat's personality, and what was discussed that evening, made a deep impression on Chandi Prasad. He and Rawat became good friends.

Inspired by Rawat, Chandi Prasad began travelling extensively in the Garhwal Himalayas. These trips to the remotest of villages, undertaken when he was on leave or off duty, brought him face to face with the lives and problems of the hill people. A desire to address these problems became a raging fire within him, and in 1960, he decided to quit his job with the bus company and work full-time for the development of the villages.

When he announced his decision to his family, they were quite taken aback, but Chandi Prasad was not deterred by their reaction. He left for Varanasi, where Sarvodaya workers were trained by leaders such as Vinoba Bhave in development tasks, as well as in keeping the peace during communal riots through a Shanti Sena, or peace brigade. In Varanasi, Chandi Prasad saw how women participated as equal partners in most of the work that was carried out and it made him forever committed to working with and for women, in any effort at development. This training period was a very significant one for him—in the bus accident rescue that came later, he exhibited many of the skills he learnt as a Shanti Sena volunteer.

The Malla Nagpur Co-operative was set up by Chandi Prasad and a few of his friends during these years. It was formed to help the hill people bid and work on the public works projects such as construction and road building, in competition with other contractors. Chandi Prasad worked as a labourer alongside his friends, and they lived as a community—working, cooking, eating together, and sharing equally the money they earned. In these years, as they bid for contracts and were paid exploitative rates by government departments, Chandi Prasd began to be increasingly aware of the role of the government, contractors and their agents in the systematic destruction of the forests and environment of the Himalayas.

Construction activity in the plains had gathered tremendous momentum. Road-building in the Uttarakhand region, where Chandi Prasad lived, gave access to remote forests and villages, so timber began to be removed throughout the region. Towns all over the country were growing as the population of India increased, and this was placing a fresh burden on natural resources. Increasingly, the hill people of Uttarakhand found that their environment and labour were being used to make the lives of people in the plains comfortable, while their own difficulties only became greater.

The mountain people did not get the benefit of more jobs, since construction work was assigned to contractors from the plains, who brought skilled and semi-skilled workers with them. They could only get jobs like hauling or breaking rocks, and were paid next to nothing. The shrinking forests began to make it extremely hard for the village women to find firewood and fodder. By the time Chandi Prasad witnessed the landslide and the bus accident in 1961, he had begun to be aware of the changes occurring in the mountains due to environmental destruction. In 1964, he and his friends from the Malla Nagpur Cooperative formed the Dasholi Gram Swarajya Mandal (DGSM), or the Dasholi society for village self-rule.

The aim of this organization was to improve employment opportunities for the mountain people through the creation of small-scale industries based on forest products and to execute community welfare projects. In the beginning, the DGSM set up a small carpentry shop to prepare wooden items and marketed traditional medicinal herbs. Then, with the help of the Khadi and Village Industries Commission, they established small factories in villages to produce turpentine and resin from the sap of the chir tree, known as lisa. In the early years, the mandal also worked vigorously against the consumption of liquor by the mountain people, which worsened the living conditions of people already poor by circumstances. In this, they had the strong and solid support of the women of the region. Chandi Prasad's wife, with whom he had a troubled relationship for some years due to his community work, also joined in the campaign, without his knowledge. When the Alaknanda river saw its worst flooding ever in 1970, the DGSM members were active in relief, rescue and rehabilitation work.

While the DGSM had been successful in creating employment for over a thousand people from 1969 to 1972, they found that they had to compete with commercial interests with far greater clout than them, who succeeded in pushing them to the sidelines.

For instance, when they began to produce turpentine, they were in competition with a big turpentine factory in Bareilly. To their consternation, they discovered that this big factory was supplied raw material at subsidized rates by the government, while they had to pay much more! This naturally put them at a disadvantage.

By October 1971, the mountain-dwellers' anger against this double-pricing system swelled to a public outcry. Chandi Prasad Bhatt became the spokesperson for the people in whose midst he had been born and had grown up to serve. After several demonstrations outside government offices and institutions, the demands of the mountain people were communicated to the government by him. These were:

- To put an end to the unfair pricing policies,
- To stop using outside contractors to provide labour, and
- Review, and if necessary restore, the villagers' traditional rights to gather forest products.

No satisfactory response, however, was forthcoming. Official replies were tardy, or did not address the issue, or sometimes, were made without any follow-up action to execute them.

Meanwhile, his prompt rescue work after the bus accident had attracted the attention of another campaigner for the mountain people's rights—Sunderlal Bahuguna. From then on, the two met and consulted each other at regular intervals, and it was through their efforts that the rest of the country and the world became aware of the ill-effects of environmental destruction in the Himalayas, and the suffering this brought in its wake.

The definitive turn in the affairs of the DGSM came in April 1973 when the people learnt that the government forestry department had given the felling rights for a large number of ash trees to Simon Company, a large sporting goods manufacturing company from Allahabad. What made the mountain-dwellers angry was that they had been denied permission by the forestry department to cut down a much smaller number of these ash trees!

Heated discussions among the mountain villagers about the best method of preventing the agents of the company from felling the trees began to take place. In the past, the DGSM had organized dramatic non-violent protests accompanied by traditional drummers and mountain trumpets. Now, some young people began to suggest setting fire to the forests, or even attacking the men who came to cut the trees. In such a scenario, it was Chandi Prasad who came up with the suggestion of hugging the trees to prevent them from being felled. 'Go into the forests, embrace the trees (Chipko!), and defy the woodcutters to let their axes fall on your defenceless backs,' he advised. But even he could not have visualized how deep the idea of this novel protest was to sink in the minds and psyche of the mountain people. The word *Chipko* came in time to signify the entire movement.

The efforts of the DGSM saw that the Simon Company left without being able to fell a single tree. They continued their vigil against planned felling in the Reni and Phata forests. But the contractors, who were working with the help of some officials in the forestry department, decided to use stealth to defy the 'Chipko' strategy of the people.

One day, Chandi Prasad Bhatt was summoned to Gopeshwar to meet a delegation of forest officials, who were suddenly showing an interest in the DGSM. On this same day, the government announced it would pay compensation to those who had suffered damages during the Indo-Chinese Border War of 1962. Payments were being made at the town of Chamoli. This prompted all the men of the region to flock to Chamoli, leaving the women and children alone in their villages. Knowing full well about the absence of the village men and Chandi Prasad, a felling contractor and his men set out for Reni forest.

The bus carrying the workmen drove with sealed windows to hide the men who travelled within. But when they reached journey's end and got off at Reni village, a small girl noticed them and reported their movements to some women. Gaura Devi, a fifty-year-old housewife, rounded up twenty-one women and seven girls to follow the men into the forest. They caught up with the workmen and pleaded with them to leave without cutting the trees, but the men shouted and threatened them. The women refused to be cowed down and when the men raised their axes, they flung themselves on the trees and embraced them, to the dumbfounded amazement of the labourers. Now they saw the power of the simple word 'Chipko!'

The labourers had to finally give in and the whole group started back along the forest track with the village women following the men. A small part of the path had a gap where a landslide had swept away the track. This was bridged by a cement slab, and when the last woman had stepped across, she dislodged the slab, sending it crashing down into the river below. The women had cut off the path to the forest to ensure that the men could not return immediately. They still, however, huddled on the path, guarding the forest till the next morning when the village men returned.

This dramatic incident provided a turning point for the

people of the mountains. It made women feel they could be fearless equal partners with the men in protecting their lives and the forests that gave them fresh air, water and fodder. It emphasized for people that they were the guardians of their own forests, not only against exploitative contractors, but also against their own fellow villagers who used the hill slopes for fodder and fuel without thinking about the consequences. It gave a fine example of how non-violent methods could be used to assert people's rights, even under extreme provocation and in the face of men with axes.

In the years following this incident, the DGSM has continued to raise people's awareness of the need to protect and enrich their own environment. They undertake reforestation campaigns to restore the health of the forests and conduct environment conservation camps where men and women, students, non-government organization members, scientists and academics work together to evolve measures to help maintain the ecological balance of the Himalayas.

Now consulted by the government on environmental issues, and attached to several policy-making bodies, Chandi Prasad Bhatt has been successful in leading a mass movement for the preservation of the environment. But in his typical humble way, he refuses to attach too much importance to his leadership. In his acceptance speech when receiving the Ramon Magsaysay Award in 1982, he said, 'In Indian mythology, the Himalaya is considered the abode of God . . . That is why God gave us inspiration to start a movement to save this wonderful creation. He made small people like us the instrument for the conservation movement. Because of the strength derived from Almighty God; the forces who were destroying the Himalaya's environment, and who had the full backing of the exploitative social system and of the law, were halted by small people of small villages. And in the front line came those simple, hesitant village women who had never crossed the boundaries of their household duties' (www.rmaf.org.ph).

Chandi Prasad Bhatt has enabled many of us to cross our mental boundaries and look at the earth and environment that sustains us with fresh eyes.

J.N. KAUL

THE ASSISTANT DIRECTOR OF THE Social Welfare department of the Delhi administration, J.N. Kaul, was used to official meetings with visiting foreign dignitaries. As a government officer, it was his job to acquaint such visitors with the schemes and projects the government was undertaking for the people's welfare. As he prepared to meet Dr Hermann Gmeiner, the founding father of the SOS-Kinderdorf movement in Germany that provided homes to orphaned and homeless children, he had no idea that the simple meeting was to be a big turning point in his life.

The two men took to each other instantly. One was a well-built Austrian, whose vision had helped save many thousands of children all over the world from the traumatic effects of natural disasters, war and other calamities. The other was a Kashmiri civil servant, whose recent course of study abroad had led to offers of employment from reputed organizations in the West.

As Dr Gmeiner talked about what SOS-Kinderdorf had been able to achieve for children in several countries of the world, his words found an echo in his companion's heart. Finally, Dr Gmeiner leaned forward to say, 'So you see, Mr Kaul, what I am seeking is a person to anchor the SOS Children's Villages movement in India, someone for whom providing a home-like environment to children left without a home is a number one priority!'

His listener looked him straight in the eye and said, 'Dr Gmeiner, I am that person!'

From that moment, the SOS Children's Villages movement was under way in India.

Every day, the daily newspapers bring us a steady flow of information about floods, earthquakes, bomb blasts, wars and other calamities that cause many hundreds or thousands of families to become homeless in some part of the world. As we look at the pictures, or read the reports of these disasters, it is natural to wonder, what will happen to the children? Who will look after the infants, toddlers and teenagers who have lost both parents and the four walls they called their home?

The SOS Children's Villages worldwide movement was started by one individual who decided to act upon this single question, instead of letting it remain a simple thought. Dr Hermann Gmeiner, an Austrian, saw around him the devastation of World War II in wartime Europe. Thousands of their families had been broken up by the effects of bombing, warfare, and refugees fleeing from one country to the other. Children were orphaned, or lost and separated from their families, and many were in need of shelter and care. Though there were many orphanages which took in such children, Dr Gmeiner's vision was different. He knew that such children would miss the warmth, companionship and caring that they had known in their own homes. He thought of a unique method of providing such warmth and family surroundings to orphaned children. He created special 'children's villages' or *kinderdorf*, as they are known in Austrian.

The first SOS village was set up by Dr Gmeiner in Imst, Austria in 1949. It consisted of individual cottages of three or four bedrooms, where nine or ten children could live under one roof, with a 'mother', a woman who would care for them and provide emotional support. The children in each of the cottages were like brothers and sisters to each other, and they went to school, played, ate and rested together like children in their own natural homes. This replaced institutionalized care with more personalized units, where natural bonds could form. Before this, orphanages implied shelter without individual care.

The SOS villages began to be set up all over Europe, and the concept soon spread to other continents in the world. Wherever and whenever large-scale disruptions of human life had caused children to be lost, abandoned or orphaned in numbers, an SOS village was set up. This provided a home-like environment to the traumatized children and set them on the path to build their own future. By the time Dr Hermann Gmeiner came to India and met J.N. Kaul in 1964, SOS children's villages existed in several European countries, in Korea and Vietnam, and in Latin American countries like Argentina, Ecuador and Uruguay.

The man who was willing to start the SOS children's village movement in India, Jagan Nath Kaul, was born on 13 October 1924 in Srinagar. One of the reasons behind his immediate response to the vision of Dr Gmeiner was that he had been a witness to the trauma and upheaval caused by Partition in 1947. Displacement of families, loss of home and property, and the effects these had on children was something he, too, had seen first hand.

J.N. Kaul studied at Punjab University after his initial education in Kashmir. After graduating, he did an MA in economics from Rajasthan University, and thereafter joined the Delhi administration in the social welfare department. It was while he was working there that the government sent him abroad for further studies in childcare. In 1963, when he met Dr Gmeiner, he was seriously considering his future course of work—several good offers had been made to him. But he knew his education, training, circumstances and own personal desire had best equipped him to care for traumatized children.

The first SOS children's village was set up in India in 1964 in Faridabad, near Delhi. It was named Greenfields, and J.N. Kaul was its director. The children promptly started calling him 'Papaji'. Two hundred children made their home here. Among them was Siddhartha, Jagan Nath's son, who found the years growing up in an SOS village so inspiring that he decided he was going to be a part of this movement in the future too. The village itself, with so many siblings and their mothers who were like his aunts, was his home till he left it to study. Today, Siddhartha is the head of SOS-Kinderdorf in Asia, helping to set up many more such villages.

From the earliest stages of his work, J.N. Kaul was able to involve eminent personalities concerned with the welfare of children in the activities of SOS. The first president of SOS villages in India was Tara Ali Baig, and Indira Gandhi lent considerable support to SOS when she was the prime minister. In fact, the Government of India has turned to SOS to provide help and succour to children in several instances, notably in Assam in 1983, when terrorist activities had affected the normal life of people in the state.

Life in an SOS village is designed to resume the reassuring, even tenor of normal family life that has been disrupted and destroyed by calamity. Children wake up, get ready for school and eat breakfast with their brothers and sisters. Their mother gives them packed lunch boxes. They attend local schools and return for an afternoon snack, followed by playtime with friends in the village, an evening spent doing homework alongside their siblings, then dinner and bed. There are plenty of celebrations around the year, and song, dance, theatre, arts and crafts are very much a part of the children's lives, lending an element of joy to the community. A father figure in the form of the director is available to deal with minor personal crises that the children may face, and the 'mothers' in charge of each of the cottages are dedicated women with affection for children, whose parenting skills have been supported by training.

The most important priority is to instil a sense of trust in children, and make them realize that they still live in a caring and kind world. It is impossible to replace everything the children have lost—parents and relations, the special space they called home, memories of the time they spent with their families. But the SOS village family often begins to mean as much to the children as their own parents once did. In fact, some of the children have chosen to live together even in their adult lives. A few of them applied for loans with the help of SOS, and built homes, where their SOS 'mothers' live and care for them even today. The official part of their mothering duties may have come to an end, but the bonds forged between children and their caregivers remain very strong indeed.

It is through the consistent dedication and involvement of J.N. Kaul that the SOS children's villages in India have retained their character, and ably fulfilled their role of building future citizens out of children whose lives have been shattered. He has been showered with innumerable awards and citations in his more than four decades of dedicated work with children, among them the Padma Shri in 2000, the Shiromani Award in 1996, the Man of the Year, Outstanding Individual and Lifetime Award for Social Service, at different times. He has been called Manav Shri, Manav Bhushan and Manav Ratnakar by different organizations that recognized him as a jewel of humanity, and has also been called a Karmayogi and Rashtra Gaurav or pride of his nation. His efforts in promoting communal harmony have fetched him the Sadbhavana award in 1996 and 1998, and the Secular India Harmony Award in 1998 given by the United Children's Movement.

But it is entirely in character that more than any of these awards, what J.N. Kaul values is the effort put into bringing back into the mainstream hundreds of children who otherwise faced a bleak future. He describes this achievement thus:

'The primary objective is to integrate them back into society. Given the right opportunity these children do very well. They have grown in the atmosphere of love and care, and about 500 of our children are happily married.

'Many of the youngsters from SOS children's villages throughout the country have completed their studies and are doctors, engineers, teachers, business managers and social workers etc. We have many success stories and are very proud of them. Fourteen of our youth from the SOS villages of Assam fought at the Kargil front in 1999. Thirty-two of our young adults have joined the Army as jawans and some have joined the Army Nursing Services.

'We are very ambitious for our children; we share their dreams and hopes and aim to eliminate fear and desperation. There have been failures just as there are many success stories. But we have never abandoned any child and never will.' (In conversation with Manisha Parikh Srivastava, www.samachar.com)

The SOS children's villages have moved fast time and again to contain the pain and anguish of children in the recent history of India. Since the movement arrived in India in 1964, it has expanded its work at a rapid pace. There are now thirty-four villages and 122 allied projects including facilities for

Tibetan children. Today, SOS provides direct care to 15,000 children through its villages and indirect care to nearly 200,000 children through its various community projects, which include kindergartens and schools, social, medical and vocational training centres and its Family Helper programmes. J.N. Kaul still serves as the organization's president in India and looks forward to the day when one of the SOS children passes the IAS exams 'and then gives up the Service, like me!'

In fact, administration officials still in the service, like district collectors and those in charge of rescue and relief operations in natural disasters, often have cause to be very grateful for the help that SOS provides for the affected children.

In 1983, when terrorist activities and communal violence took a toll in Assam, many children were rendered orphan and homeless. SOS established two children's villages at Bhakatpara and Hojai to take care of these children. Its presence in Assam has been increased with one more children's village at Guwahati and several youth facilities.

The very next year, 1984, saw a great environmental tragedy occur in Bhopal. Thousands of people died due to leakage of poisonous gas from the Union Carbide factory. Hundreds of orphaned children found a home in a newly established children's village at Bhopal, set up specially for this purpose.

In September and October 1991 two devastating earthquakes affected the lives of thousands of people in India. In September, the village of Latur in Maharashtra and its surrounding areas were hit by a powerful earthquake that caused immense loss of life and property. In October, the epicentre of the earthquake was in Uttarkashi, in the Himalayan foothills of Uttaranchal. SOS set up a children's village at Latur, which is functioning even today, as well as kindergartens and day-care centres. At Uttarkashi, the affected children were taken to the SOS village in Bhimtal, which was already running at that time.

The severe cyclone that struck the Andhra coast in November 1996 led to the setting up of a village at Vishakhapatnam. The government of Andhra Pradesh was deeply appreciative of the efforts of SOS India. Another cyclone that struck Orissa in October 1999 was a call for SOS to swing into action there. Affected children were placed in the existing children's village in Bhubaneswar. The work done during this crisis was appreciated so much by the Orissa government that they allotted land free of cost at Rourkela for SOS to set up another village in the state, and find place for more orphaned and homeless children. Apart from natural disasters and calamities, children also come to SOS villages referred through hospitals, government-run homes, police authorities, railway authorities, social workers, and friends of SOS.

Man-made disasters have played their part in disrupting the social fabric, depriving people of homes and families, and causing widespread misery and anguish. Terrorist activities in the states of Punjab and Jammu and Kashmir led to two SOS villages being established at Jammu and Rajpura (Punjab). SOS is also addressing the problem of rehabilitation of young people forced to migrate out of Jammu and Kashmir. A large number of such young men and women are being trained in various trades to make them stand on their own feet.

In a dramatic instance of intervention, SOS was called in by the government of Andhra Pradesh in June 1999 to take care of 228 infants under the care of two Inter Country Adoption Agencies, allegedly involved in child trafficking. These children were given shelter in a centre opened at Hyderabad, which is being developed into a full-fledged village. This has since been pointed out by various experts as an example of excellence in childcare.

J.N. Kaul's personal leadership and exemplary qualities are often very much in evidence, as in the instance when Gujarat was struck by an earthquake in January 2001. Massive death and destruction marked the epicentre of the quake, but SOS workers, led by J.N. Kaul, commenced immediate relief work in the worst affected areas. Within a few weeks of the earthquake, twenty-five Emergency Child Relief Centres were set up in Anjar, Bhachau and Bhuj. In the beginning, SOS provided day-care services to around 2,500 children in these centres, including midday meals, education, play and therapeutic arts and theatre. These centres greatly helped to reduce the trauma of the children at a time when families were temporarily disrupted and schools were not functional. Out of these children, those who would require permanent care were identified, and were given a home. Before an SOS village was set up in Gujarat, SOS mothers and their co-workers began SOS families for these children in temporary shelters and rented accommodation in the badly affected towns of Bhachau, Anjar and Rapar. Subsequently, an SOS children's village has come up in Bhuj, with fourteen families.

The parent organization of SOS-Kinderdorf, donors, sponsors, friends and well-wishers contribute to the projects of the SOS children's villages of India. The organization has succeeded in touching a chord in the hearts of the larger public. Programmes and events that bring SOS activities in the public eye are conducted from time to time. Larger infrastructural costs like construction of cottages are met with help from the international organization and other donors.

J.N. Kaul believes, 'One of the reasons for the success of our projects is our ability to meet the accountability factor. We have both internal and external audits and we apply modern management techniques and principles in the functioning of the organization. There is total transparency in the functioning and the overall idea. The success and growth is mainly on account of four reasons: strength of a powerful idea, accountability, transparency and friends of the children who are committed donors and sponsors of our projects' (www.samachar.com).

Today, thousands of homeless children have benefited from the vision of Dr Hermann Gmeiner, and the dedication and leadership of J.N. Kaul, affectionately known to everyone in the SOS family as 'Papaji'.

ELA BHATT

THE WOMEN WERE DRESSED IN tattered rags. Their skirts, blouses and dupattas, or their saree pallus, had the telltale holes of poverty and neglect. 'How ironic that they should be thus dressed, in the heart of Ahmedabad's cloth market!' thought Elaben Bhatt. As she sat on the steps of a warehouse and listened to them pour out their woes, it was as if a dam had burst, and their pent-up emotions had at last found release through expression.

'The load on my head is so heavy that I suffer from a continuous pain in my neck and back,' said one woman.

Another had a child clinging to one hip. Her slender frame seemed fragile, yet she worked in the cloth market all day. 'Some days the seth sends us away without wages, saying he has a cash shortage! How can we help if he does not have money to pay us? We need the money to cook dinner for our families!' she pleaded to Elaben.

'They use us just like donkeys,' grumbled another woman. 'As if our bodies are only good for carrying cloth from the wholesale market to the retail one. As if we are not human, and we have no feelings!'

Elaben's own feelings were threatening to overcome her. As the head of the women's wing of the Textile Labour Association (TLA), she had accompanied the migrant women who carried head-loads in the textile market to their houses and places of work. She wanted to understand their problems better. But the depths of misery, poverty and exploitation in which they lived affected her so strongly that she became determined to fight for a better deal, not just for them, but for the millions of self-employed women struggling against odds in the city. As the women continued talking, late into the dusk of an evening in

1971, Elaben's conviction to do something for them kept growing. It did not matter what obstacles she would now encounter. She would do what she could.

Awareness of social issues, and a desire to do something against exploitation and injustice, was a part of Ela Bhatt's family tradition. She was born on 7 September 1933, in Ahmedabad, where Mahatma Gandhi had spent many years after returning to India from South Africa. Ela Bhatt's family—her father Sumant Bhatt, and mother Vanalila Vyas, as well as her grandfather and uncles—were all influenced by the Satyagraha movement of Mahatma Gandhi.

Upholding the rights of the poorest in society, and resisting the cruelty and injustice of authority was part of the fiercely Indian spirit that prevailed at that time. Ela's father, grandfather and uncles were all lawyers, and her mother was active in organizing women through the All India Women's Conference. Ela's maternal grandfather, a doctor, was jailed several times for his participation in Satyagraha protests and fasts. The child Ela grew up in an atmosphere where her nearest and dearest always discussed issues affecting fellow countrymen and women.

Ela attended school from 1940 to 1948 in Surat, a bustling industrial town on the western coast of India. Her father had a successful law practice in this town, and she continued her studies by attending college here as well. It was while she was studying for a Bachelor of Arts degree in English that Ela volunteered to work in the national census of 1951. This participation brought her face to face with the vast numbers of people living in extremely poor and miserable conditions. While going door to door, and seeing first-hand the struggles of workers and their families to merely survive, Ela had decided about her life's work. She knew that she would devote her life working to better conditions for these people.

During her college days, she met Ramesh Bhatt, who helped her give shape to some of her thoughts and ideals. She and Ramesh were married in 1956, and have remained partners to this day, wedded to common concerns. As a student leader and Gandhian, Ramesh encouraged her to work for the neglected and underprivileged. Ela went on to study law after her graduation, partly in response to her father's desire that she become a lawyer. In 1954, she received a law degree, with a gold medal for outstanding work on Hindu law. But she did not immediately begin work as a lawyer. For a year, she taught at the SNDT Women's University in Mumbai, before moving to Ahmedabad in 1955 to join the legal department of the TLA.

For the next several years, Ela Bhatt worked as a lawyer appearing in the labour court on behalf of textile workers. The TLA had grown out of the textile workers' strike of 1917. It was founded by Anasuya Sarabhai, Shankarlal Banker and Mahatma Gandhi. It represented a model union for workers in that period, even those from other cities and industries. Ela Bhatt learned a lot as she fought cases on behalf of the workers, and described her work as 'a compromise between social work and legal work'. Later, she took a short break from work when her children were born, and she was busy with the care of her two small children, born one year apart, daughter Amimayi and son Mihir.

From 1961 to 1967, Ela was employed by the labour ministry of Gujarat, where she performed different functions at different times. She initially worked towards providing suitable candidates to employers, then went on to provide vocational guidance and training of candidates in addition to job placement. When she was appointed Incharge of Occupation Information from 1966 to 1968, she explored new employment opportunities, reviewed existing definitions of various occupations, and framed definitions for new jobs.

In 1968, the TLA called her to rejoin the union as head of its women's wing, which undertook training, production, unionization and research. Health and welfare measures, training women in stitching and embroidery, and marketing their products were all part of the TLA effort.

In 1971, Ela Bhatt went to Israel to study at the Afro-Asian Institute of Labour and Cooperatives in Tel Aviv. She saw that every sector of Israeli workers was unionized. Even the wives of workers had their own union, and thus, each group was well represented, and had a voice to put forward their needs.

Returning home, Elaben (as she was called by her colleagues and those whom she represented in the TLA) was struck afresh by the plight of women who arrived in the city from villages, worked to provide essential services and faced extreme hardship. Elaben met many women who toiled daily to make Ahmedabad a comfortable city—as vegetable vendors, handcart pullers, milkmaids and junk collectors who collected old iron and tin articles and reshaped them into usable goods. She saw that they were poor, vulnerable, and had no bargaining power against employers and authorities. Laws may exist to protect the interests of workers, but Elaben found, to her distress, that the 1971 census had not even classified these toiling women as 'workers'.

Elaben decided to work for the interests of these self-employed women. The surveys conducted into the conditions under which they worked and lived revealed great deprivation.

Women who pushed, rather than pulled, handcarts with loads of 500 to 700 kg, often had their babies strapped to the underside of the carts. Bhatt's book *Profiles of Self-Employed Women* (1975) describes many of these women who sold milk, used garments, recycled iron and scrap articles and vegetables. She found that 97 per cent of these women lived in slums, 93 per cent were illiterate and their average number of children was four. Their monthly incomes (in 1975) ranged from Rs 50 for the garment makers to Rs 355 for the vegetable vendors. Many of these women were steeped in debt, as they had to take loans from moneylenders just to survive. All of them worked under crippling handicaps like a shortage of money to invest into their trade, shortage of raw materials, an uncertain workplace and murderous interest rates on money borrowed for daily rents of transport or buying of stock.

The women's wing of the TLA could not encompass all the different occupations that made up the poor and vulnerable self-employed women of Ahmedabad. The women urged Elaben to work for their interests, and in consultation with Arvind Buch, the president of TLA, she launched the Self-Employed Women's Association (SEWA) in December 1971.

The first obstacle that presented itself was in getting SEWA registered as a trade union which would be a recognized body to represent the interests of its members. The labour department initially refused to register SEWA as a trade union, saying that the women were 'self-employed' so there was no employer for the women to petition for their cause! Elaben and her fellow SEWA organizers pointed out that a trade union did not exist only to plead against an employer, but also to form workers into a united front to solve their common problems. They succeeded in convincing the authorities and SEWA became a registered trade union in 1972.

An early triumph for SEWA came from their representation of the women who rolled beedis for a living. They were scattered all over Ahmedabad city and made the beedis in their homes. These women collected the tobacco and leaves, with which to make beedis, from traders who paid them on the basis of the number of finished pieces they provided. Traders would often reject bundles of work on flimsy grounds, then buy these at a lower rate. The families, particularly infants and young children, of the beedi rollers came in contact with tobacco and beedi materials, since the women had to work in the cramped space of their own huts. They also worked at a lower than minimum wage and had no access to free medical facilities in case of illness. Each time they tried to demand a better deal from the traders, they were cowed down by aggressive words and threats. SEWA moved in to organize the women and was able to show them the strength of the collective. When the women, united in spite of living in far separated areas of Ahmedabad, stood up against the traders in 1971–72, the traders had no option but to yield. A better return on the workers' hard labour was made possible by their collective bargaining.

SEWA was drawing members from all categories of daily earners in Ahmedabad. With a membership fee kept deliberately low enough to be affordable for the poorest, it grew into an organization that represented home-based workers like beedi workers, quilt makers, readymade garment makers and agarbatti makers. It also had members who were manual labourers and service providers such as construction workers, handcart pullers, coolies, ragpickers and workers in small factories.

Many poor women in and around Ahmedabad made quilts, pillows and children's garments out of scraps of cloth that were leftover pieces from the main wholesale and retail markets. These scraps, called *chindhis*, were bought in large quantities at very cheap rates by prosperous traders, who sold them in small lots to the women. The women had to work hard in their tiny ill-lit homes to make finished products that were bought back by the traders. The traders paid them paltry wages, and made handsome profits on the scraps as well as the finished product.

SEWA workers began organizing the women quilt and garment makers into a cooperative. 'Why not buy the chindhis for your needs directly from the textile mills, and sell your products through a cooperative shop?' they suggested to the women, who responded enthusiastically to this idea. But as the group of women tried to take direct control of the chindhis, they met with plenty of resistance. The traders and textile mills attempted to deprive the women of the chindhis altogether, so that they would not be able to obtain the raw material for their craft.

After a determined struggle against this monopoly, the women gained access to the cloth, and learnt to transport their raw material and finished products, operate a cooperative shop, and keep accounts of all the transactions.

From the very beginning, the SEWA executive committee members comprised self-employed working women. This made it a truly empowering organization for the poorest and most neglected sections of society.

In 1979, the struggles of the vegetable vendors brought Elaben directly in confrontation with the city authorities and residents. Fresh vegetables are liked and sought by all, but those who make a living selling them are seen to be a nuisance, and city 'beautification' campaigns often push them to far-off areas where they find it difficult to carry on their trade. Even on a daily basis, they are harassed by the police, who demand sums of money from them as bribes, or by moneylenders from whom they borrow money at exorbitant rates of interest, just to buy their daily stock. Elaben found that these vendors' lack of any legal status made them especially vulnerable, and she began to make efforts to get them vending licenses and identity cards. This had some success, but the bigger struggle was yet to follow.

In Ahmedabad, the vendors sold their wares in and around Manek Chowk, one of the oldest and biggest markets in the city. When a brawl broke out between two people in the crowded market one day, and others too became involved in the violence, the city authorities imposed a curfew, which stretched on for days. Elaben and SEWA appealed against the curfew, since the vendors' lives had come to a complete halt, but their appeals were ignored. Finally, they decided to defy the curfew!

As Elaben described it in an interview to Mirai Chatterjee in www.rediff.com, '. . . we decided to break the curfew and practice civil disobedience. We asked the vendors to bring their goods for sale in the market. The decision was that if the police came, SEWA organizers would face them before the vendors. We arrived in the market at eight in the morning. Four police vans were already in position, as if they feared violence. The police approached and began reasoning with me. We were a bit worried because more than the regular customers, we expected some trouble from goondas. But as soon as the women began selling, the whole market started humming with business as before. The police came to me and said, "You don't seem to be concerned—even when elders like Mr Buch have advised you, you are still persisting with breaking the curfew. What about your self-respect and status in the city?" I told them that I didn't care about such things, about my status and so on.

'The police were a bit taken aback by my firm stand. "What if there is trouble in Manek Chowk market?" they asked. I said, "We'll see to it that there will be no trouble." I don't know what they discussed on their wireless, but suddenly they withdrew from the scene. All of them. It was noon by then. We continued to sell in Manek Chowk for five days.

'For those five days, all of us managed the traffic. Business thrived till late at night. And the vendors were able to enjoy full sales—no cuts to anyone, no police inspectors, no fear of confiscation of goods, no running away from the authorities. Good business without any fear or tension. We then came to an agreement with the authorities and organized a campaign around this incident.'

Elaben, by her fearless support of the marginalized people of the city, has forced other city dwellers to look differently at the impoverished service providers around them. Her work has not only been effective in changing attitudes and perceptions, it has brought many concrete gains in thousands of lives. She and her SEWA colleagues had been very concerned about the plight of women who pulled and pushed handcarts loaded with over 500 kg weight piled on them. SEWA took the help of LD Engineering College and the National Occupational Health Institute, to design a cart that avoids excessive strain on abdominal muscles. In the old carts there was constant friction between its handles and the abdomen of the women or the thighs of the men. The specially designed cart could be pushed by women in a more comfortable posture and had additional features like extra space for carrying a baby underneath, as well as a braking system.

The most remarkable institution to come out of the SEWA movement has been the Shri Mahila SEWA Sahakari Bank, a cooperative bank that was started in 1974 with a contribution of Rs 10 from each SEWA member. This bank has succeeded in freeing thousands of women from the debt trap in which they lived earlier when they borrowed money from moneylenders to buy daily necessities. The bank is managed and run by women who had to first practise writing their own names when they started the bank! But these women have shown that they are equal to the educated and trained staff that are employed in other banks. The loans given to thousands of self-employed women have had an excellent repayment record. The women have proved that they need just a little help in their daily conduct of business, and their hard work and acumen is enough to do the rest.

The many institutions that SEWA has built up in the last three decades include ninety cooperatives, the Mahila Bank, federations and SEWA branches in many other cities, national-level trade facilitation such as Saadhan, Friends of Women's World Banking, Mahila House Trust, and Women's World Trading. SEWA is also organizing insurance cooperatives for women. In 2003, the annual turnover of SEWA cooperatives was Rs 18 crore, and the SEWA bank is able to earn a consistent dividend of 15 per cent. SEWA members, from the daily wage-earning segment of society, put back Rs 1.5 crore into the local economy daily. All these facts bear witness to Ela Bhatt's dream of bringing about a Doosri Azadi or Second Independence for women through economic self-sufficiency.

In September 2003, when she was awarded the Economic Times Award for Businesswoman of the Year, Ela Bhatt said, 'When we began, I realized that till economic freedom reached the common man, political freedom would not mean much. The rich had always had access to the capital markets, not so for the poor' (*Economic Times*, 18 September 2003). Ela Bhatt has done her utmost to ensure this access for the poor. Much recognition has come her way—the Ramon Magsaysay Award for Community Leadership, the Padma Shri, a Lifetime Achievement Award from FICCI, and innumerable felicitations.

But for Elaben Bhatt, the greatest reward is simply this— making managers, leaders, articulate businesswomen and respected artisans out of women who once wore tattered rags.

BINDESHWAR PATHAK

'HOW CAN A NATION CELEBRATE the birth centenary of a great man without making efforts to remove the miseries of those people whom he had befriended?'

This question was often in the mind of a wavy haired student of Patna, who had been greatly inspired by the ideals and values of Mahatma Gandhi. Not a day went by without his being a witness to the plight of those Harijans who had received special attention from Gandhi in his crusade against untouchability. The year was 1968, and all over the country, preparations were on to celebrate the birth centenary of the Mahatma, who had played such an important part in the formation and identity of independent India.

The values that Gandhi had upheld were firmly embedded in Bindeshwar Pathak's heart. The sight of sanitation workers, or bhangis as they were called by their north Indian brethren, was one that, he felt, called for immediate attention. It was a shame that certain people had to physically remove human excreta and waste from public gutters, and worse, that they were looked down upon by other members of society as 'untouchables'. Why were these people still in extremely pitiable conditions? Were they not the very same that Mahatma Gandhi had tried to uplift and strengthen? Mahatma Gandhi had worked hard to give them back their human dignity, even as he tried to make people aware of the need to maintain hygiene and cleanliness.

All these thoughts drove the student to join the centenary celebrations in his own special manner, by joining the Bhangi-Mukti (scavenger's liberation) cell of the Bihar Gandhi Centenary Celebrations Committee in 1968. While the nation was soaked in images and words from Gandhiji's life for a whole year, the young student spent the entire time travelling, eating, sleeping and working alongside the 'untouchable' sanitation workers.

Often, the sanitation workers looked at the idealistic student in wonder. 'What will you do with all you have learnt about us?' they would ask him. Bindeshwar would give different replies at different times, but his determination grew stronger with each passing day. He knew he had to work as hard as he could to improve these people's lives. He knew this had to be done even if it meant battling with the attitudes of society at large.

Let us save them from squalid conditions and in doing so we'll be saving the national conscience, was his thinking.

His vision and genius gave birth to a movement called Sulabh or easy, a sanitation movement that simultaneously aims to restore human dignity, promote health and hygiene, protect the environment, and manage waste for future resources.

The sight of men, women and children defaecating in the open is something that all of us are exposed to at some time or other in our country. Especially around cities, this sight is all too common, as slum dwellers use open public space by the side of railway tracks, or around river banks and water sources, as toilets. For most of us fortunate enough to have a comfortable home with each bedroom equipped with an attached bathroom, such sights produce more revulsion than sympathy. But the problem of bathing, defaecating and urinating in the open is one that is a daily part of the lives of millions of our countrymen.

To Dr Bindeshwar Pathak, who grew up in a privileged Brahmin household, this sight represented the most urgent call to action.

Bindeshwar Pathak was born on 2 April 1943, in a village

called Rampur Baghel in the Vaishali district of Bihar. He graduated in sociology, and by the time he was part of the Bhangi-Mukti cell of the Gandhi centenary celebrations, a highly developed social conscience had already convinced him that in tackling the problem of waste management and disposal, he could address human issues as well as scientific ones.

Two years after his personal participation in scavengers' lives, Bindeshwar Pathak came up with the design of the Sulabh Shauchalaya, or toilet. With this simple design, he was determined to change the sanitation and public hygiene scenario of the country. He launched the Sulabh Shauchalaya Sansthan in 1970. This later became the Sulabh International Social Service Organisation. The newly designed toilet was at first greeted sceptically by people, some of whom openly jeered at the concept. But this was not going to stand in Bindeshwar's way. He was used to his ideals and inspiration being rejected and ridiculed—even his parents and family had not taken kindly to his long association with the Harijans.

The Sulabh toilet that Bindeshwar Pathak conceived is a very simple device. It consists of two pits and a sealed cover. While one of the pits is in use, the human waste in the other pit is left to turn into manure. This technology removes the need to physically clean the excreta. Initially ridiculed, the Sulabh Shauchalaya was declared a global Urban Best Practice at the Habitat-II conference held at Istanbul in 1996. In fact, recognizing that the Sulabh technology can be a boon for the poor and deprived in many developing countries, the Economic and Social Council of the United Nations granted Special Consultative Status to Sulabh International in recognition of its outstanding service. Appreciation also came from another important quarter. 'You are helping the poor,' lauded Pope John Paul II while honouring Bindeshwar Pathak with the International St. Francis Prize for the Environment, in 1992.

The ingenious Sulabh toilet can be adopted in different terrains and conditions with some precautions, and can be put in place by local people. Its low-cost and people-friendly technology found popularity and recognition among those who needed it the most—poor rural and urban dwellers, who have no access to proper toilets or conveniences. For it to be accepted on such a large scale, Dr Pathak had to convince administrators, planners and engineers about the successful functioning of its two-pit system. The pour-flush toilet was found to be an affordable, safe and hygienic system for the disposal of the human waste in the absence of sewers and septic tanks, ideal for urban areas, where human population is so dense. Before this, nobody had believed that this technology could work in cities, and no engineer or technologist had patented it.

When Bindeshwar Pathak first began his work, he had set out to prove that humans handling and clearing the excreta of their fellow beings was not a practice sanctioned by the scriptures of Hindus. This was needed in order to change social attitudes, and stop exploitation of sanitation workers in the name of tradition. In fact, this was something that Mahatma Gandhi had also tried to point out. In addition, Dr Pathak also saw waste management as an important weapon to face future power shortages. Sulabh is the first organization to tap the potential of biogas from human waste.

Dr Pathak has always emphasized the importance of toilets in maintaining public hygiene and health. Throughout human history, devastating epidemics and destructive diseases have swept populations when animal and human excreta have polluted water sources and places where food is grown or stored. As Dr Pathak says in his direct and forceful manner, 'Toilet is a critical link between order and disorder. The subject of toilet is as important, if not more, than other social challenges like literacy, poverty, education and employment. More important, actually, because lack of excremental hygiene is a health hazard.' (www.sulabhinternational.org)

Dr Pathak's concerns are still relevant in our country, where open defaecation remains a reality for millions many years after independence. Women bear the brunt of problems caused by lack of toilets and water. They often have to bathe and dress behind flimsy partitions, or leave well before sunrise, or after sunset to defaecate in the open. Every day, over 150 million Indian houses function without toilets and over 10 million other houses use bucket toilets which spread filth and disease. This directly contributes to the conditions that cause about half million children to die every year due to dehydration caused by communicable diseases. It is such harsh conditions that led Dr Pathak to declare some years ago, 'Nobody should go outside for defaecation, and every house in India should have a toilet.'

How could the health and hygiene problems of the community be addressed through a provision of proper toilets without astronomical sums of money being needed or spent? Dr Pathak's ingenuity had the answer.

In 1974, the community toilets that have since become a trademark of Sulabh International, were launched for the first time. Each such toilet has bathing, urinal and laundry facilities, with attendants in service around the clock, and is operated on a pay-and-use basis. The first such toilet was opened in Patna, and since then, over 5,500 toilets have been established in cities across India. Electricity, twenty-four-hour running water, separate enclosures for men and women, and a standard of cleanliness have made these complexes popular with the public wherever they have been set up. Some of them are also equipped with shower stalls, first-aid kits and primary health care facilities and telephone kiosks.

When the Sulabh technology began to be adopted in more and more towns, over 50,000 sanitation workers from more than 240 towns were liberated from their task of working closely with excreta, and were resettled into other professions by Sulabh. More than 10 lakh houses that had been using bucket toilets converted to the Sulabh pour-flush system over some years. By the year 2000, Sulabh had a presence in 338 districts in twenty-five states. They even had a toilet complex in Bhutan. Over 50,000 people man the Sulabh offices and toilet complexes around the country. Close to 1,100 community toilets service thousands of Indians around the clock in busy urban areas.

As the Sulabh movement began to gather momentum, Dr Pathak turned his attention to the problems of those with whom he had shared many moments of laughter and camaraderie, as well as loss, and sometimes, despair. He had studied the lives and conditions of sanitation workers with thoroughness and dedication. He did his PhD in 1985 on the subject 'Liberation of Scavengers Through Low-Cost Sanitation'. This was followed by a DLitt study in 1994, 'Eradication of Scavenging and Environmental Sanitation in India—a Sociological Study'. In the course of writing his papers, he observed that scavenging as a community profession was practised in many times and places. Yet thoughout history, scavengers remained a special class united in their miseries. Thus, providing toilets was only one part of the cessation of the suffering of sanitation workers, so long considered as 'untouchables'. Equally important was finding alternative occupations for them, and changing social attitudes towards them and their families, which would enable them and their children to work for a better future.

It was to address these urgent issues that Sulabh International set up a number of vocational training institutes. Former scavengers and their family members, as well as other persons from deprived and disadvantaged backgrounds are trained at these institutes in various vocations like computer technology, typing and shorthand, electrical trade, woodcraft, leather-craft, diesel and petrol engineering, cutting and tailoring, cane-furniture making, masonry work, and motor driving. This makes it possible for some of the most poor and neglected persons from our society to gain new means of livelihood, rise above poverty and enter the mainstream.

This change in their areas of work needs to be bolstered by the confidence that comes from education. Recognizing the importance attached to the use of English in our society, Dr Pathak set up an English-medium school in Delhi for children of sanitation workers, a pioneering effort of its kind. Here, half the number of children come from sanitation worker families and the rest from other communities. Through this coexistence and co-education, the deprived children have the opportunity to interact with their peers on equal terms, something essential to prepare them for a better life. The Sulabh school makes quality education affordable for boys and girls from families where education has remained a dream for many generations.

In order to make people more sensitive and accepting towards sanitation workers, Mahatma Gandhi declared in the beginning of the twentieth century, that 'the Bhangi is as important as the Viceroy'. He embraced Harijans, who had lived for centuries under the scourge of untouchability, shaming the rest of his countrymen also into a gradual acceptance. But the discrimination against the lowest strata of our people, represented by the sanitation workers, is so deep-rooted that its ill-effects are visible even today, in the twenty-first century. Bindeshwar Pathak works with the same vigour and conviction for a better and egalitarian society as he has done for providing clean and affordable toilets.

In 1988, he took a hundred of these so-called 'untouchables' and some Brahmins to the famous Nathdwara temple in Rajasthan in a clear demonstration of social upliftment and integration. Since 1993, Sulabh has been working on another plane of social harmony and acceptance. Dr Pathak made a heartfelt appeal to privileged families to interact with at least one family of sanitation workers. His appeal was aimed at the roots of discrimination and exploitation in our society, which prevent the lowest castes and communities from aspiring for a better life, and the wholehearted acceptance of their fellow humans.

One of the first people to respond to this appeal was India's then prime minister I.K. Gujral. His warm gesture of adopting a sanitation worker's family showed the way to others. Over 5,000 families of sanitation workers have been affected by this programme, which enables the voluntary acceptance and involvement of the powerful with the least empowered. Sulabh is working to extend this in a phased manner throughout the country.

It is a remarkable characteristic of many leading social activists, that their work continues to extend itself in many directions, after the original initiative has established itself. In Dr Bindeshwar Pathak's case, there are two distinct streams in his work and philosophy. On the one hand, he is concerned about using technology and science to improve the lives of people. On the other hand, he is committed to social reform—to improve the society and world around him by changing people's attitudes and removing their ignorance. The wonderful thing is that he has worked for these goals over the last thirty years and more, without seeking personal recognition and fame for himself. In fact, the brand name 'Sulabh' is far more easily recognized all over the country than Dr Pathak's own name.

The Sulabh technology continues to search for solutions to improve the health–environment–hygiene scenario in our country. In a path-breaking effort, Sulabh International put forward the idea of obtaining biogas from human excreta collected in large-sized public toilets used by 2,000 to 5,000 persons each day. The first such biogas plant was set up at Patna in 1982 after almost six years of research. Since this plant was a success, the project could be extended to sixty-eight centres all over the country. Today, biogas plants connected to large-sized public toilets are operating successfully in many towns. Through this initiative, Sulabh demonstrated a future method of human waste disposal, and a source of renewable energy.

Other important developments from the continuing research and experimentation conducted by Sulabh are production of biogas from dried and pulverized water hyacinth plants, obtaining granulated organic manure from the dried sludge of biogas plants, and preparing of compost from solid waste within five or six days, without human handling. The Sulabh International Institute of Technical Research and Training (SIITRT), set up in 1984, is responsible for these developments, while the Sulabh International Institute of Health and Hygiene (SIIHH) and the Sulabh International Institute of Rural Development (SIIRD), both situated at the Sulabh Bhawan in New Delhi, work directly with the public on projects for the common good.

The Sulabh Museum of Toilets in New Delhi houses information and artefacts relating to toilets since 2500 BC! Collected with the help of volunteers in over fifty-six countries, the museum has many interesting exhibits such as the commode that French king, Louis XIII, had installed under his throne, and another that is disguised as a library of books. Apart from being a fascinating collection of sanitation-related objects and curiosities, this museum also provides us some very important information. It talks of the grim harvest of death when proper sanitation was not observed in times of war, or during epidemics and natural disasters. It reveals that the Indus Valley civilization in our country had houses with toilets equipped with individual water closets. That is how much the early inhabitants of the subcontinent were concerned with cleanliness and sanitation. More than 4,000 years later, close to 700 million of our countrymen have inadequate toilet facilities, simply because we have not chosen to give sanitation the attention it needs. An encyclopaedia of sanitation is also being compiled under the leadership of Dr Pathak.

Health and hygiene are inextricably linked to proper sanitation. In our country, sanitation has also been tied to social issues such as the discrimination that has been practised against sanitation workers. Most of us see one end of the problem, rather than the composite whole. It takes a compassionate, clear-eyed and courageous leader like Dr Bindeshwar Pathak to point the path for us all.

ARUNA ROY

THE APRIL SUN WAS ALREADY very warm on the heads of the hundreds of villagers assembled in Gomti Chauraha of Beawar town in Rajasthan. Tents erected around the area were meant to shelter the villagers in the nights for the duration of their stay. Thirty-seven of these were already filled, and people still continued to pour into the town from the 300 and more villages in the area.

In the colourful and picturesque state of Rajasthan, where tourists jostle each other to take pictures of the turbans and moustaches of men, and the multi-hued ghaghras and chunris of women, a passer-by could have been forgiven for thinking this was another of those village fairs.

But if he or she listened closely to the groups talking animatedly among themselves, he or she would have noticed some important differences. Firstly, women and men talked to each other freely in a way different from the usual gender-based segregation in villages. Secondly, their conversation revealed far more serious concerns than the sale of camels or a village feud.

'For just ten villages, between 1994 and 2000, the amount they have managed to divert from actual use is Rs 45 lakhs!' said one villager.

'And that is from only thirty-one projects studied from the ninety-eight they had announced,' said another voice, this time a woman's.

'If the tally is Rs 45 lakhs diverted from 1 crore even without half the projects being examined, then just calculate what will be the final score!' said another villager excitedly.

In response to this, the assembled group raised a slogan, *'Roti do, naukri do, nahin to gaddi chhod do!'* (Give us bread, and give us jobs! If not, get out of that seat of power!)

Clearly, this was no routine celebration marking the passing of a season in festive Rajasthan. It was a Jan Sunwai, or public hearing, called by the Mazdoor Kisan Shakti Sangathan (MKSS). In April 2001, the villagers around Beawar had assembled to mark five years of their movement for the Right to Information.

In another thickly packed group of villagers in animated discussion, a slightly built, saree-clad woman sat listening attentively to what the villagers were saying. 'Now that the official records are in our hands, we have a very powerful case for the corrupt officials' arrest,' she said in a quiet voice when the group turned to her for guidance at one point. The assembled group responded with exclamations, grunts and approving murmurs. The villagers were perhaps still doubtful of the official machinery that would have to move to arrest the corrupt officials who had robbed public money marked for development, but they had no doubt at all about the ability or determination of MKSS leader Aruna Roy. She was a woman who had travelled a long way to get here.

Official budgets, that earmark money meant to be spent for the public good, are a routine feature of our lives. They are announced daily through newspapers, television reports, and even on posters and hoardings in big cities, put up in praise of one or another leader. If we listened closely to these announcements, and kept a tally of how much money has been supposedly spent in improving roads, sanitation, public health and education, we would indeed wonder why India is still a 'developing' country. Why do large sections of Indian people have to live in such abject poverty, when every passing day brings some official scheme or project to improve their lives? The official figures of expenditure, and the reality we see before our eyes every day, present a completely contrasting picture.

We hear only too often about the 'corruption' that goes on around us. But what form does this corruption take, and how does it harm us? And more importantly, how can we, along with our fellow citizens, put an end to corrupt practices?

Those of us who live in cities do not find it very difficult to go about our work, because the facilities and services that enable us to function are maintained by governments, most of whom are also based in cities and towns. In rural areas, people face much tougher challenges in obtaining the basic necessities of their lives—clean water, electricity, roads and transport to other villages and towns, medical facilities to take care of the sick, and the proper distribution of food grains and rations. While misappropriation and misuse of public funds happen in both urban and rural areas, in the villages they take a much more life-threatening form. People can die from lack of basic medical facilities, or starve due to improper food distribution. Members of the administration who divert public money for their own profit are indeed criminals who must be brought to book and given harsh punishment.

Administrative officials and elected representatives in our country are able to misuse public funds and ignore the aspirations of the people because we rely too much on elections to keep our democracy going. While elections are certainly the most visible method of ensuring popular participation in the governing of a country, they are certainly not the only sign of a democracy. For a country to be truly democratic, its citizens should understand the processes that govern their lives, and be free to question these processes when the need arises. Only in this manner can the performance of the administration and the elected representatives who head it, be evaluated by those who have brought such people to power.

The MKSS is an organization that has worked for the people's Right to Information since it was formed on 1 May 1990. Aruna Roy is one of its founders.

Born in Tamil Nadu in 1946, Aruna Roy grew up in the Delhi of newly independent India, while the country was still coming to terms with the trauma of Partition. She was a lecturer in English before she joined the Indian Administrative Service, or IAS, considered a 'plum' vocation in middle-class India. She married Sanjit 'Bunker' Roy, who had set up the Social Work and Research Centre (SWRC) at Tilonia, Rajasthan, in 1972. An alumnus of Doon School and St Stephen's college, Sanjit Roy had worked in several social work and development jobs after completing his postgraduation in 1967. He decided to work exclusively in rural India after coming face to face with the effects of a devastating famine in Bihar. The Barefoot College he had set up in Tilonia educates and empowers rural people by equipping them with livelihood skills and helping them develop appropriate technology.

Since 1972, two generations of villagers without any formal qualifications have been trained in this college to become health-care workers, solar engineers, hand-pump mechanics and teachers in their communities. The SWRC at Tilonia has enabled over 1,00,000 people in 110 villages to have access to safe drinking water, education, health and employment. This has been achieved through the active participation of rural youth, once regarded as lacking any marketable skill, who install and maintain solar electricity systems, hand pumps and tanks for drinking water. Traditional artisan skills are upgraded at special workshops. About 3,000 children from the area attend night school, to receive a non-formal education that allows them to stay as useful and contributing members of the rural community, rather than become 'educated aliens'.

Aruna Roy worked as an IAS officer from 1968 to 1975, but the security of her job did not compensate for what she perceived as the wrong way of doing things. As she explains it in an interview, 'I could not get rid of the nagging doubts and the sense that something was not right. As officers, we met the rural elite. Even a good collector, I later learnt, does not and in fact cannot permeate the unwritten code of rural India's ethics on who may, or may not meet the officers. And of course, the public places where such meetings are held, are often designed to keep the poor, the Dalits and women on the outer peripheries' ('Learning With Equality—Redefining Gurus', www.humanscape.com).

When she decided to leave the IAS and apply herself to development work in the rural areas, it was natural that she should come to Tilonia, where SWRC was already showing powerful results. The next nine years were spent in learning to work at the grass-roots level. As she has engagingly described in 'Learning With Equality', Aruna Roy, with her urban and privileged upbringing, had to grow out of all the preconceived notions she had arrived with about villages and about rural society. She saw the divisions along gender and caste lines among rural people, and the courage and indomitable spirit of many individuals who rose above such divisions. She saw the concerns and priorities of the people, and how the administration rarely addressed them.

From her work in Tilonia and her close interaction with Dalit communities, she learnt that 'economic development alone could not solve problems at the grass-roots level'. In order to bring about long-term change, people need to have access to the institutions and processes that govern them. Rural society provided Aruna with the opportunity to perceive the strength and wisdom in collective leadership. She also saw the need to enforce accountability of individuals and institutions engaged in governance and development.

In 1983, she left the development work she had been engaged in at Tilonia. It was time, she felt, to move on and define for herself what form her future work would take. It seemed inevitable by now that she would become more 'activist' and less 'social worker'. How the transition would be made remained to be seen. In 1981, she had met Shankar Singh, an extremely talented theatre personality gifted with the ability to communicate with people at various levels. When Shankar Singh made the decision to actively join the social struggle, and Nikhil Dey, a young postgraduate also wanted to be engaged in this, Aruna decided to move to Devdungri village in the Rajsamand district of Rajasthan in 1987. Here, Shankar Singh and his family, Aruna Roy and Nikhil Dey lived, convinced that 'most of the answers to the questions we had lay with the people themselves'. In complete contrast to her initial apprehensions about village life when she first arrived in Tilonia, Aruna Roy lived in a hut and kept a goat. She still lives and works alongside the rural people to whom she gives the credit for shaping her struggle.

'Many collectives of the poor people struggling for change gave us the ideas and the commitment to bring about meaningful change. In fact, this has been one of the outstanding lessons of my twenty-five years of work in rural Rajasthan. I owe my ideas to the clarity of others; my courage to being with people who confront injustice with fearlessness and equanimity; my hope to the persistence and resilience of men and women struggling to get themselves heard; my generosity to the poor family that shared its last roti with me and my sense of well-being to the many who have supported me in difficult moments of my life.' (Interview with Kamala Bora 'We can't all be Gandhi or Mao', www.rediff.com).

The MKSS was born out of an agitation for minimum wages by poor and illiterate rural workers who worked on government projects and were regularly denied their rightful wages by government officials, with the argument that 'according to our records, these people have not worked'. These records were kept locked in government offices. The affected villagers felt that making these records available for the public to examine would prevent contradictory claims by officials and workers. In short, the rural people were demanding to see clear evidence to support the claims of government officials. They understood that secret records prevented them from identifying when officials were carrying out policies that did harm to the people.

This understanding of the rural people was proved true in an unexpected way by the disclosure of an official enquiry report. It revealed that a bogus company, Bhairon Nath and Sons, had received payments for labour that had never been done! The company itself was traced to government employees from a small town called Bhim. Obviously, these men had set up a fictitious company, and doctored the government records for their own gain. Moreover, the government auditors had cleared the expenses of Rs 36 lakhs even though the company had no record of having paid sales or income tax. It was evident that the fears of the rural people about official records being a big stumbling block in their development were truly justified. What was needed was to ensure that such records were open to public scrutiny.

In 1994, the MKSS was approached by a worker from a village called Kot Kirana in the Pali district of Rajasthan. He wanted their help in getting the rightful wages he was being denied. The organization agreed to help on condition that he would demand access to records covering the entire period of his employment. He agreed, and the groundwork began to bring details of official expenses into the public arena.

A sympathetic official in the administration allowed details from an inquiry report to be noted by MKSS, and they began visiting the rural people door-to-door, pointing out instances in the government records that clearly showed misuse of money marked for public purposes. Instead of adopting the usual agitational path of leading people to government offices manned by unsympathetic staff, MKSS adopted the Jan Sunwai method. This allowed concerned people to gather at one place, have an open debate about what the official records had revealed, and chart out a series of steps that should be taken to set things right. The first such Jan Sunwai was held in Kot Kirana on 2 December 1994. It raised the following demands:

• That all public works and accounts be made transparent,

• That a people's audit be held to assess the accountability of the administration, and

• That a system of redress be set up to manage the return of money that had been illegally diverted.

The overwhelming response that the Jan Sunwai generated led to MKSS conducting a series of such meetings from December 1994 to April 1995. By April 1996, they had raised enough awareness on these issues to launch the Right to Information campaign from Beawar town. The campaign began with a forty-day dharna in the town by MKSS activists, along with large numbers of rural people. Warmly welcomed and accepted by the local community, Aruna Roy and her colleagues, Nikhil Dey and Shankar Singh, found their morale restored by the people when their own spirits flagged. As Nikhil Dey described it, 'In the forty-day Beawar dharna (sit-down protest) in April-May 1996, we had 400 signatories to the campaign. We got free vegetables for the community kitchen, free videography, and dharamshalas (rural rest-houses) opened their doors for us. A small child gave us two rupees every day and flower-sellers gave us five rupees daily out of their sales, while the chaiwallah (tea-vendor) gave us tea at half-price. These are just a few instances of solidarity that gave us hope and energy' (Deepak Mahaan, 'Transparency and Poverty in India', www.worldpress.org).

Fresh enthusiasm in the campaign was also infused by the humour and irreverence employed by Shankar Singh to illustrate the grim reality that had sparked off the Right to Information movement. A Ghotala Rath Yatra by a typical politician figure who considers himself to be above all questions, invariably drew much laughter and appreciation from the assembled crowds.

The sustained campaign by MKSS and the people of rural Rajasthan led to the passing of the Rajasthan State Right to Information Act in 1996. Following this, MKSS continued to hold Jan Sunwai meetings wherever instances of large-scale misuse of public money were identified. Some of these were at

Umarwaas village in Udaipur district, where they exposed the misuse of public funds in the execution of a public works project in December 1999, and Janawad village of Rajsamand district in 2000–01.

Subsequently, the state governments of Delhi, Goa and Maharashtra have enacted Right to Information Acts, and the Indian Parliament has enacted a Freedom of Information Act.

Aruna Roy was awarded the Ramon Magsaysay Award for Community Leadership in 2000, an honour and prize money that she immediately dedicated to the 'ordinary people' of Rajasthan in whose midst she has lived and worked for close to three decades. Her life and work have been immeasurably enriched by them.

'There is a notion that people's attitude could be changed through training and development more fundamentally than through struggle. In the MKSS I found that struggle is a greater and quicker equalizer. There is a desire to change which arises out of ground realities. The people are far more practical in defining the limits of struggle and drawing lines . . . These are people who have little formal education and are economically poor. What is clear, however, is that the poverty is not of their minds or of their hopes at all. So in their battles against their conditions of poverty, one has had an opportunity to recognize the richness and texture of their commitment to, and understanding of their own struggles. They are fully capable of dealing with their lives, if they could find some space. The MKSS continues to search for such spaces' ('Learning With Equality—Redefining Gurus').

In enabling large numbers of her fellow citizens to demand accountability from the people who govern them, and in consistently resisting the use of public funds and resources for private gain, Aruna Roy has helped strengthen the democratic fibre of our country to no little extent. As she says, 'By casting a vote, we accept our share of the responsibility for shaping and controlling the system of governance. We cannot shrug off that responsibility for five years until the electoral process begins all over again. Questions need to be asked consistently since accountability is a continuing process,' ('Transparency and Poverty in India').

SUGATHA KUMARI

GREEN FORESTS TEEMING WITH LIFE and hope are often a source of inspiration for writers and poets, who seek shelter in them to be refreshed and rejuvenated. Merely reading poems written about forests and nature can refresh readers and listeners.

But as one particular poet looked at the stark and barren landscape of Attapady in 1984, her mind was thrown into a tumult of sorrow and anger, then despair, and finally, determination. The hilly, predominantly tribal area of Attapady in north Kerala, once green and lush with vegetation, now resembled a desert. Denuded hills exposed the dry channels of what had once been sparkling waterfalls. Deforestation, soil erosion, and the takeover of tribal lands by people who did nothing to regenerate the forests they had destroyed, had pushed the area into the destructive arms of heat and dust. As the wind blew over this bleak landscape, it threw up spirals of dust. These dust devils seemed to be particularly malicious, as if mocking the poet. She felt as if they were daring her to do something for this land and its people.

'Only by greening this area again, by rejuvenating its dead forests, can the lives of the tribal people be saved,' she thought to herself. 'Why should they be pushed into poverty and beggary, subject to the whims and fancies of politicians, government officials and middlemen? Bringing the forest back to life will give them the resources they need to live a decent life once more.'

From this call, which had risen directly from her heart, the poet made a decision to take up a small area of now denuded forest and attempt to revive it. In her typical fashion, she threw herself into this task with a lot of energy and enthusiasm, assisted by friends and like-minded people.

The magical greening of Attapady had just begun.

Sugatha Kumari, the celebrated Malayalam poet, was born in Thiruvananthapuram in 1934. Her father was a freedom fighter, and in the years of struggle against British rule, Sugatha learnt many lessons of patriotism and sacrifice. More importantly, since her father was also a poet, she grew up to understand how significant social ideas could be communicated through creative expression.

Growing up to write poetry herself, Sugatha Kumari challenged many conventional ideas of the society around her. Her refusal to stay silent in the face of any form of injustice earned her the reputation of a 'troublemaker'. The literary establishment was awakened to the qualities of her strong woman's voice, and her poems began to acquire their own following, and she became one of the leading contemporary poets in Malayalam.

Sugatha Kumari was plunged into social activism with the struggle against the building of a hydro-electric plant planned in the forest area of Silent Valley in 1970. This irrigation and electricity project would have led to the destruction of many hundreds of hectares of virgin green rain-fed forest in Kerala, home to many rare species of wildlife as well as herbs and medicinal plants. Concerned about what such destruction could mean for Kerala, Sugatha Kumari persuaded a group of her fellow poets and writers to bring these issues before the people. They organized a series of prakriti mushairas, or nature poetry gatherings, for the public. On these occasions, the debate of modernization and development versus environmental conservation was conducted through the language of poetry, touching the hearts of people, rather than merely appealing to their minds.

The Silent Valley project was the subject of much controversy.

Dr M.S. Swaminathan, appointed by the government of India as head of a task force to examine the viability of the project, urged the government of Kerala not to go ahead with its plans. Several other organizations, like the Kerala Shastra Sahitya Parishad and the Bombay Natural History Society, also recommended the same course of action. But in the end, what led to the project being abandoned was the strong public resistance that had built up to its execution. This resistance was undoubtedly strengthened by the poems and writings of Sugatha Kumari and her friends. Indira Gandhi, then prime minister of India, also lent her personal voice to the cause of environmental conservation.

A few years later, when Sugatha Kumari stood and gazed upon the barren waste that Attapady had become, she was facing an environmental challenge of another kind. Would it be possible to reverse man-made damage through concerted effort?

Sugatha Kumari formed a group called the Prakriti Samrakshana Samiti, with poet N.V. Krishna Warrior as its president. This group prepared a project proposal for Council for Advancement of People's Action and Rural Technology (CAPART), an organization that disburses funds from the Government of India. Finally, they received permission from the government of Kerala to work on an area of 100 hectares of denuded hills around Bhoomiyampathy village. This village had hills on three sides, all of which had turned brown after being deforested. Shrubs, ashen grass clumps, and hundreds of old tree stumps completed the picture of devastation.

The tribal people had once lived here in dense forests that yielded honey, fruits and tubers for their nutritional needs. Water, firewood, food grains, medicines and materials to make their homes and dwellings had been available from the forests. They revered and respected these forests, and put back what they received, by ensuring that the forest never suffered irreparable damage.

When people from towns and cities began encroaching on tribal lands, they cut down trees and burnt the undergrowth. Cattle was allowed to graze indiscriminately, so that, in between the stumps of trees, even the grass was gradually destroyed, leaving bare hillside.

The destruction of the forests that sheltered and supported them affected the tribal people in a devastating manner. They fell into abject poverty. When the Prakriti Samrakshana Samiti first began talking to them, they found that most of the girls did not attend school at all, and even those children who went to distant government schools often dropped out. The adults had become daily wage labourers after their earlier lifestyle was destroyed. In their despair, many of the men had taken to drinking and alcoholism had become rampant among the community.

Faced with this depressing scenario, the Samiti decided that their first task was to motivate the tribals and make them partners in the effort to green Attapady. They asked the old tribal chiefs to describe the forests as they had once been, and unlocked the treasure house of knowledge that these people carried within them. With the help of the tribals, they set up a small hut of mud, bamboo and thatch. This became the office of the Samiti, and every evening the tribals assembled here. While their children ate a nutritious snack and played in the clearing in front of the office, the adults talked to Samiti members. They discussed the importance of having forests again, of education, and how alcoholism was destroying them and had to be resisted. The evenings played an important part in bringing the Samiti closer to the tribal people—to the women who were 'efficient and hopeful', and the men who were sometimes 'moody and lazy', according to Sugatha Kumari.

In the courtyard of the Samiti office, a nursery of seedlings was started, of trees native to the area. Thousands of small pits were dug on the denuded hillside with the help of the tribals and kept ready for the seedlings that were to be planted. Cattle and sheep grazing was totally prohibited, and a thorny fence of kaitha plants was put in place all around the planted area to protect it from stray grazers. Help from the community was also enlisted in the shape of fire-watchers—volunteers posted to prevent the spread of bush and grass fires that could destroy precious undergrowth. To ensure that rainwater did not run off the hillside without irrigating the seedlings, the channels and gullies on the hillside were plugged with stones and bush. Now the rains were eagerly awaited.

Attapady is in an area of Kerala adjacent to Tamil Nadu which depends on the north-eastern monsoon which hits the area in October and November. It receives hardly any rain in the June to September season. After the pits had been dug, as soon as the first showers had wet the land, the adivasi men and women and the members of the Prakriti Samrakshana Samiti worked to plant the seedlings in the soft earth. The mood was one of great enthusiasm—the tribals sang as they worked, and in each heart soared the hope of a greener and better future. Apart from the pits that received seedlings, many were left open to receive rainwater, and act as natural storehouses. In addition, many sackfuls of seeds collected from distant forests were scattered over the moist hillside. No effort was spared to pour these into the welcoming earth, each with its precious potential for blossoming into a plant, or a tree.

The effects were quite dramatic. As Sugatha Kumari describes it, 'Slowly the barren hills responded and began to look green. Most of the seedlings took root and began to grow and we saw to our immense joy that where we had planted a hundred seedlings, a thousand unknown plants and trees were coming up as if touched by a magic wand. We planted a thousand bamboos, and lo! a ten thousand came up! We had scattered seeds and the birds also took up that work. Most of the old stumps of cut down trees began to sprout leaves. Slowly a small woodland began to take shape in front of our eyes.

'It was in the third year of our work that an adivasi watcher came running to me with a happy announcement: "Amma, a barking deer has come to our forest." A deer which had escaped some hunter's bullet had sought refuge in our newborn forest. "See that nobody harms it," I told him. "He is our first deer." But luckily "he" turned out to be a "she" and after some months the tribals rushed to me with glad tidings: "Amma, a baby is born to our deer . . . we heard its cry." Now we have a herd of barking deer in our forest. For our woodland has become a real forest after some seven years. It has everything—trees, creepers, clusters of bamboo, small wild animals and birds of all hues. A tiny stream has sprouted which disappears in summer but comes out laughing when the rains come. Adivasis take honey from the beehives, they have fruits and medicines, bamboo and firewood and proudly proclaim, "This is our forest. It was dead, we made it reappear" ' (From Sugatha Kumari's account, 'How to Green a Dream').

The experience at Attapady had placed Sugatha Kumari firmly at the heart of ecological and development issues. It was thus that she received the Vriksha Mitra Award, in addition to literary honours like the State Sahitya Akademi Award, and the Central Sahitya Akademi Award. In October 2003, she received the prestigious Vallathol Literary Prize for her 'outstanding contribution to Malayalam poetry'. This prize has been instituted in memory of the veteran Malayalam poet Vallathol Narayana Menon, and Sugatha Kumari was receiving it on his 125th birth anniversary.

Another direction to Sugatha Kumari's activism was to unfold after her reputation as a poet and environmentalist was already well established. Once, on a chance visit to the government-run mental hospital in Thiruvananthapuram, she saw how women patients were housed and treated. The horrifying spectacle seemed straight out of the nineteenth century. There were women with matted hair, and sores and scabs covering their naked bodies. To her horror, she discovered that these starving and emaciated women also suffered sexual abuse, sometimes at the hands of the police from a nearby police camp. Even in this first moment of shock, Sugatha's resolve did not desert her. She was determined to do something about the plight of these mentally ill and destitute women.

Shockingly, the hospital authorities and the psychiatric establishment in Kerala were initially bitterly opposed to Sugatha Kumari's attempts to bring some dignity back into the lives of these unfortunate women. They denounced her in public, and continued to display the 'We-are-professionals-we-know-what-we-are-doing-so-don't-challenge-us' attitude. But Sugatha was undaunted, and gathered sufficient activists, intellectuals and politicians to force the government to institute an inquiry into the condition of mentally ill patients in government-run hospitals.

Meanwhile, she also began collecting food, items of clothing and other necessities for distribution to the women in the hospitals. Out of this practical drive to improve conditions for the women, an institution was born. For the first time, the attention of the public and the judiciary was focussed on the pitiable conditions of the mental hospitals of Kerala. Having succeeded in opening the hospitals and their functioning to public scrutiny, Sugatha Kumari also came forward to offer a model of care and shelter in the form of Abhaya, an institution she set up with some associates in 1985. Abhaya is not only engaged in advocacy work for better care and treatment of mentally ill patients in government hospitals in Kerala, it also provides care to women in distress, mental patients, alcoholics, drug dependents, and the children of parents in high-risk groups.

A number of care and counselling centres have come up under Abhaya. Athani is a short-stay home for women who are in distress because of being battered at home, who have been deceived or duped, and women who have tried to run away from homes due to sheer poverty. Athani provides medical, legal and psychological help for women to regain their self-respect and make their way back into the outside world. Skills are also developed for them to be able to earn a living. This has been sponsored by the Central Social Welfare Board, and there is a women's helpline attached to Athani, where any woman in distress can call and ask for help around the clock.

Bodhi is a counselling and de-addiction centre set up by Abhaya in 1988 with help from the Government of India. This has inpatient as well as outpatient care for victims of alcohol and drug dependence. Doctors, counsellors and social workers work with the patients and their families to rehabilitate them back into productive lives.

As part of their efforts to improve conditions in government-run mental hospitals, Abhaya runs a centre in the mental hospital at Thiruvananthapuram called Pakalveedu. Music, excursions, exercise, occupational therapy and vocational training are offered here to patients who are about to be discharged from the hospital, or those who have already been discharged.

The National Fund for Rural Development of the government of India enabled Abhaya to buy ten acres of land on the outskirts of Thiruvananthapuram in a village called Manchadi. This is the site of Abhayagramam, the focal point of several of Abhaya's multifaceted activities. Karma is a centre that functions from Abhayagramam, giving free treatment, care and skill development training to mentally ill patients. Woven items and crafts made from bamboo and banana fibre are some of the products these patients make at Karma.

Mitra, also housed in Abhayagramam, is a mental health and de-addiction centre for those suffering from mental disorders and substance abuse. Modern drug therapy, behaviour therapy, individual, group, marital and family counselling make Mitra a very special centre. Since patients pay for services provided by Mitra, it also functions as a support system for all the other units where service is given free.

Abhayabala is a home for children who have gone through some of the most harrowing experiences in their short lives. Initially begun as a shelter for daughters of the inmates of Athani, Abhayabala now has over sixty bright and energetic girls who attend school, and sometimes also join vocational courses. Three resident teachers supervise their educational and creative activities. Abhayabala is a cheerful place, and described as Abhaya's 'hopeful tomorrow'.

As the busy and energetic secretary of Abhaya, Sugatha Kumari today still grapples with many of life's problems. She has a deep understanding of how social attitudes and beliefs contribute to the creation of social ills, and her determination to do something to bring sanity and compassion into the social mainstream remains as strong as ever.

In fact, what makes her impatient are many fatalistic beliefs that still exist among us, that extreme difficulties and handicaps are a result of bad 'karma'. Such an attitude is usually an excuse to sit idle, she feels. Inspired by the Gita that exhorts us to fight, to struggle, to be active rather than passive, she says, 'If we can wipe the tears of even one woman, it must change her karma as well as ours.'

In her lifetime, Sugatha Kumari has successfully wiped away many such tears, giving many individuals a reason for hope.

RAJENDRA SINGH

THE MORNING RAYS OF THE sun beat down upon the retreating backs of Satyendra, Kedar, Hanuman and Narendra. As he watched them walk away from where he stood, in the shelter of a small temple, Rajendra Singh's eyes were filling up with tears, his mind was confused and stunned. How could this have happened? A few weeks ago, they had all arrived together from the city of Jaipur. Their bus had reached a small village called Kishori, in Rajasthan's Alwar district, late at night. They were five friends with a single desire—to work for the development of the rural community in which they had arrived.

When they had got off the bus, they were leaving behind lives of comfort in the city, determined to do something to improve conditions for the rural folk who lived in great hardship and poverty. Their sudden arrival at night had created a stir among the villagers. Some even suspected them to be a gang of terrorists or kidnappers! They were given shelter for the night in a small Hanuman temple by a kindly priest. And there they began to stay.

The friends had left home on 2 October 1983. Inspired by Mahatma Gandhi's ideals, they were looking for a path to put these ideals into action. Thus, on his birth anniversary, they set off to work in rural areas to better the lives of people. They arrived from Jaipur, intending to work towards providing better education and improving living conditions. These were the areas where they felt their own education and experience would prove useful.

But immediately after their arrival, as soon as they woke to the rural dawn, it was clear that the greatest problem people faced in this particular region was the availability of water. The scarcity was so acute that young men had left to work in the cities, unable to carry on farming on their family land. The elders were left behind, as were the women. The women had the most difficult time imaginable, just to cook and feed their families. Daily, they trudged many kilometres to distant wells, where a thick rope would have to travel several hundred feet into the ground to bring up a half full bucket of water. This water was poured into pots and carried back home. It was barely enough to cook and drink. Bathing was a luxury attempted only once in a while, as was washing clothes. Apart from all the hard work that went into carrying the water, most of the village women worked at another daytime job—breaking stones in quarries, to be able to earn some money for food. The few heads of cattle that the people tended looked starved and weak. Their grazing lands had shrunk to near nothingness.

The five youths from the city began to meet and talk to the villagers. On their very first day, they found several children suffering from diarrhoea, and they helped their mothers make a salt and sugar solution with which the children could be saved from dehydration. Rajendra Singh gave some medicines to a few very severely affected children. Some children had already succumbed by then to dehydration. After their initial suspicions about the young men vanished, the rural people began to talk to them, particularly an old and respected member of the village called Mangu Patel.

Mangu Patel threw a challenge at the youths, 'If you want to do something for us, work to get us water!' His words struck a deep chord in Rajendra Singh, who recognized the connection between water scarcity and all the other suffering that came as a result. Mangu Patel also told the young men about the traditional 'johad' tanks that had been a feature of each village for centuries. These man-made depressions in the ground were used to store rainwater and provided drinking and irrigation water for the community. But many years of neglect had led to them becoming dry, filled with soil and rocks, and a dismal reminder of the arid conditions. The more the youths discussed this with Mangu Patel and others, the more convinced Rajendra Singh became that reviving the johad tradition was necessary to bring prosperity and health to the villages of the area.

'We came here to try and build schools and clinics, but it looks as if we should be building johads instead,' said Rajendra Singh to his friends. After many animated discussions on the topic, it was decided to begin work on one such johad with the help of the villagers. A date was set and announced, and all the villagers were invited to come and contribute their effort to the task of creating a small-sized lake. The night before the digging was to begin, Rajendra Singh could not sleep for quite some time due to a mixture of excitement and apprehension.

He awoke before dawn and approached the temple priest to assemble some spades and basins in which to carry away dirt and gravel. Soon his friends had also arisen, but when they gathered together, Rajendra Singh received the greatest shock. They had all decided to return to the city! 'We came here to make use of our education,' they said, 'not to do physical labour to make tanks! We think you are straying from the path we had set for ourselves, so we have decided to go back.'

Rajendra Singh could hardly believe his ears. How could they turn back now? What would happen to the promise they had made to the villagers, their appointment to begin the digging?

He remained silent as his friends gathered up their belongings and began to walk away. This was truly the loneliest moment in his life.

He went inside the temple and spent a few moments in prayer. Strangely, in spite of the shock he had received, his resolve to work for the johad was stronger than ever. In a little while, he collected the spades and basins and walked to the site where the johad was to be built.

There he received his second shock of the morning. Not a single villager had arrived to help in the digging. As he stared at the silent expanse of dry mud and thorny scrub all around him, Rajendra Singh's mind cried out with the question, 'Why is there not a single person here to contribute to something that can help all of them?'

A moment later, he had shaken off this question too. He rolled up his sleeves and began to dig, completely, consciously, alone.

For many weeks, the villagers would pass him daily, as he stubbornly dug the ground. Some would whisper to each other, some others would avert their eyes. But no one stopped to help. Then one morning, Kajauri arrived and stood before Rajendra Singh. 'Give me a spade, Bhaiya,' she said. 'Let me help, too.'

Kajauri was a young mother of two children whose husband had been forced to live and work in the city because of the water scarcity. She lived with her elderly father-in-law and worked in the stone quarry. On the first day of the arrival of the youths from the city, her child had been sick and was one of the infants Rajendra Singh had helped with medicines and a salt and sugar drink. Now she wanted to return the kindness. Kajauri's extended hand of help was the signal for many others. Soon her friend Jamburi arrived to work. It seemed as if a great wall of indifference had broken down. Determined to make adequate payment for their work, and wondering how to let women do such hard physical labour, Rajendra Singh soon found that women here showed courage, generosity, and a physical strength to match their agile wits. In Kajauri's train came many other men and women.

The story of Rajendra Singh, and Rajasthan's johads began to gather force . . .

Rajendra Singh was awarded the Ramon Magsaysay Award for Community Leadership in 2001. This prestigious Asian award honours the 'greatness of spirit shown in service to the people'. By the time Rajendra Singh received the award, the efforts of the organization he leads, the Tarun Bharat Sangh (TBS), had succeeded in greening the landscape of the entire Alwar district in Rajasthan. They had repaired over 3,000 traditional johad tanks, and created more than 7,500 new ones, small dams, ponds and anicuts. These efforts had produced miraculous results, the best-known of which is the rebirth of the river Arvari.

This river had gone dry several generations back, although the ancient stone steps leading to the water and the houses built on the river banks continued to be reminders of its existence. When the residents of Hamirpur, Bhanwata, Kolayala, Paidyala and other villages began work to build johad tanks in the vicinity of their villages, they had no idea that they would succeed in recharging the groundwater to such an extent that it would feed into the dry river bed, and make the river flow again! A mere three or four years after work began in the 500 sq km radius of the Arvari river's basin, the monsoon rains filled the hundreds of village tanks, and brought the first sign of life in the river.

Soon, the flow had become strong and fish could be seen in the clear waters.

What was most amazing was that in its earlier incarnation, the Arvari had been a seasonal river, dwindling to a trickle in the dry seasons. But now, due to the hard work of the community, and the leadership and determination of the TBS, the river changed to a perennially flowing one—there was water in the Arvari all year round.

Such a dramatic and visible change could never have occurred if Rajendra Singh had admitted defeat in those first few difficult days, when it seemed his friends and the villagers, had turned against him. He stayed on, and worked, and won over everyone. In fact, the friends who had left on that autumn morning returned some years later, to become his associates once again!

Rajendra Singh's desire to do something for the society in which he was born came out of the experiences of his childhood in Uttar Pradesh. He was born on 6 August 1956, in Daula, a village near Meerut, into a zamindar family. His harsh and authoritarian father disapproved of Rajendra playing with the poorer children, but his friends were very dear to him, particularly one boy called Gopal. Gopal was the son of a poor farmer, and when he had to leave the village with his family, Rajendra was heartbroken.

Rajendra completed school and began his university education. He graduated first as an Ayurvedic physician, then did postgraduate studies in Hindi. It was while he was still in college that a significant incident occurred that left a mark on him. One day, during college hours, Rajendra's class was rudely interrupted by screams and shouts of agony. These came from a slum nearby, where a cluster of huts made of very inflammable material, like wooden sticks and thatch, had caught fire. Such fires often sweep across slum colonies in Indian towns. But Rajendra's teacher, Professor Mishra, encouraged his students to help the people whose homes were being destroyed.

As Rajendra and his friends struggled to salvage what they could from the leaping flames, a great wave of compassion for the poor daily wage earners was sweeping over Rajendra. The meagre belongings of the people, their vulnerability, the tough conditions in which they lived, all this affected him. 'Surely our people deserve a better life than this,' he thought. His friends and he then banded together to form the organization called Tarun Bharat Sangh to help rehabilitate the victims of the slum fire. They collected clothes, medicines, vessels and food for distribution. This was the seed from which the later massive banyan tree—the water-providing TBS—would be born.

Rajendra's parents were very happy when he landed a government job with the administration in Rajasthan. They wanted to see him settled, and his marriage to Meena took place. The couple set up house in Jaipur, but Rajendra found it difficult to be part of a system that he felt was not sensitive to the needs of the people. The conditions in which people lived in the rural areas he toured made him very conscious of the work that needed to be done.

It was at this juncture that his childhood friend Gopal came back into his life through a chance encounter. Both were overjoyed to have found each other again. They spent every free moment discussing their ideals. The thoughts and work of Mahatma Gandhi and Jayaprakash Narayan had a deep influence on them. Bringing about a transformation in the lives of rural people seemed to them essential to India's development. They began to plan how they would together work towards these ideals. Through Gopal, Rajendra met Satyendra, Hanuman, Kedar and Narendra.

But tragedy struck soon after. Gopal died of cancer of the liver, and an anguished Rajendra made the decision to complete the work that his friend had dreamt of, but which was left unfinished due to his untimely death. When he made the decision to resign his job and move to the rural areas for development work, his wife was alarmed, and left for her parents' house. Rajendra sold all his belongings, and after a painful scene with his father, turned towards realizing his dreams.

Along the journey, there have been many dramatic moments, many twists and turns that would have daunted a lesser man. Just as his friends returned to Rajendra, so too did his wife. She is a dedicated companion now, who has almost single-handedly brought up their two children, son Maulik, and daughter Renu, in Jaipur, while Rajendra has been busy working in the villages and attending meetings all over the country. His children accompany their father whenever the demanding schedule of school and college permits them, and are growing up to share his ideals.

There have been several physical attacks on Rajendra Singh, and one, a gunshot missed him by a hair's breadth. This is because the work of the TBS has often brought it into confrontation with vested interests. When Rajendra Singh began working among the villages around Sariska, the wildlife sanctuary, he had to confront poachers, and mine owners whose quarries had considerably damaged the environment within the reserve. The combined efforts of the villagers restored the watersheds within the sanctuary, which was a boon for both humans and wildlife. The villagers also began campaigning against quarrying, which was taking a toll on their health, as well as their environment. This was the origin of the near-fatal attack.

It is not just by providing water that the TBS has helped the people among whom it worked. From the beginning, the group would undertake to build a johad in a village, provided that the residents paid one-third of the cost of the project, and gave up liquor! This immediately had a good effect, and made people feel that they collectively owned the tanks they had built. In addition, the TBS also built schools for the village children, and trained women in self-sustaining activities like weaving, mirror work and embroidery, sheep raising and dairy farming. As the landscape across thousands of villages in Alwar, Jaipur, Dausa, Sawai Madhopur, Karoli and Jodhpur districts of Rajasthan began changing from brown to green, it brought a wave of hope and happiness among the hard-working people, tested for centuries by harsh natural conditions. It was the efforts of Rajendra Singh and the TBS that enabled people to point to not just the Arvari, but four other rivers, and say, 'Here runs a river,' then add, 'We made it!'

So much have the people of rural Rajasthan been inspired by their Rajendra 'Bhaiya' that dreaded dacoits like Nadaan Singh have renounced a life of violence and resumed an ordinary life of farming under his direction. Rajendra was also the most awaited guest at the weddings of Kajauri's son and daughter.

In his youth, Rajendra Singh invested every last rupee he had in the development work he had undertaken. Over the years, other organizations have come forward with financial help for the TBS from countries like Sweden, Switzerland, the Netherlands, Germany and others. The government has also assisted some projects. Besides, the work done by the TBS has been an inspiration to groups and individuals all over India, and elsewhere in the world.

From the end of 2002, Rajendra Singh is engaged in taking the issue of water closer to people in cities, towns and villages in India, as part of the Rashtriya Jal Yatra. Several other groups and leading activists engaged in water-related work are conducting meetings under this banner. Wherever these are held, Rajendra Singh tirelessly explains issues around the conservation and proper use of water, the community ownership of water resources, the need to resist private exploitation of water and other issues of environmental and social importance. Views and accounts of their experiences are invited from all participants at such gatherings.

In the past eighteen years, Rajendra Singh has worked to spread the ideals of environmental preservation, revival of healthy traditions, self-respect and self-determination. In the songs that the people of Rajasthan sing, he and his friends are referred to as '*Johadwale, bade dilwale*'—the big-hearted ones.

Rajendra Singh's heart indeed contains compassion for all the poor and struggling people of India.

SANDEEP PANDEY

It was May 1991, and the University of California campus at Berkeley was filled with the buzz of students and research scholars finishing term papers and projects, or making plans for their summer vacation still a month away. V.J.P. Srivatsavoy, a scientist and post-doctoral research fellow in chemistry, had organized a meeting.

For some weeks now, he had been trying to start and sustain a discussion group among the Indian students at Berkeley. Srivatsavoy was not a scientist so immersed in his scientific study that he had not noticed social realities. As a researcher in a developed country, and coming from India, he felt a responsibility towards his countrymen that he wanted to share with other Indian students. He wanted to initiate a discussion about how Indian students abroad could help the country of their birth in the areas of education and technology that was appropriate for the people's needs. A few meetings had been concluded without much emerging from them in terms of actual directions to take. On this particular day in May, he hoped something more concrete would emerge.

It did.

At this meeting, the question of 'How will we contribute to India?' gathered more strength and steam. Dinesh Verma expanded his idea, mooted in a previous meeting, of a network of personal computers (PCs) across the country which people could access and obtain information related to development. Arun Ahuja grew animated talking about making educational videos that would communicate directly to people and also serve as tools in the hands of individuals and institutions working for development. Srivatsavoy put forward his idea that professionals from various fields should be linked in an 'open-ended' network, and their skills should be pooled to work for development. Sandeep Pandey reiterated what he had been saying from the very beginning. 'We should contribute towards the education of poor and underprivileged children in India,' he said. 'Only then can we help bring in lasting social change.'

By that evening in May, an action group had emerged from the discussions and meetings that Srivatsavoy had organized. Its declared aim was to work for the education of poor children in India. Its preliminary constitution and aims were drafted by Deepak Gupta, Sandeep Pandey and V.J.P. Srivatsavoy. Its name? A very simple one, signifying 'hope' in nearly all the Indian languages—Asha.

For many Indian students, continuing their studies abroad, particularly in the United States, is an attractive option. Every year, thousands of students seek admission into universities in the US, the United Kingdom, Canada and Australia. Studying at scenic and well-landscaped campuses, and earning degrees that have international recognition is a strong enough reason for this trend to persist even in the face of India's development in the last several years. Higher education abroad is a luxury— it allows you to concentrate on intellectual pursuits, while pushing to the back of your mind the extremely deprived conditions under which so many Indians live. For that matter, most students in India too choose to stay cocooned in their individual pursuits. Intent on getting an education and a job, they forget that for many young Indians like them, an education or a job are beyond their wildest dreams.

Sandeep Pandey was born nearly two decades after India became independent. His family being comfortably off meant that he could aspire to study and work at the best educational institutes. He got a degree in science from Benares Hindu University, where he studied before leaving to do his PhD in mechanical engineering from the University of California at Berkeley. Here, his friend Deepak Gupta and he often talked about how different things were at home from the environment they now found themselves in. While he was in California, a report prepared by experts from the Massachusetts Institute of Technology (MIT) was published that revealed that more than 50 per cent of Indian children remained totally uneducated—schooling was a luxury for millions of Indian families. These findings affected Sandeep deeply. The conviction grew in him that lack of education was the biggest stumbling block for Indians to realize their true power and potential. By the time he met V.J.P. Srivatsavoy, the need to make education the highest priority in any development effort was already crystal-clear to him.

Asha symbolized the hope and optimism of the three founders who started the group on distant shores, determined to make a difference back home in India. It also stood for the hope they wanted to kindle in the hearts of Indian children by enabling them to receive an education. Asha's mission is 'To catalyze socio-economic change in India through education of underprivileged children'.

Asha found an immediate acceptance in the community of Indian expatriate students in the US. In the very first year of its existence, Sandeep, Deepak and Srivatsavoy raised ten thousand dollars for educational projects in India. Soon after, Sandeep left America and took up a teaching assignment at the Indian Institute of Technology (IIT), Kanpur. Initially, it appeared to be a good way for him to keep in touch with the projects and activities Asha had initiated. But one and a half years later, in 1993, Sandeep decided that 'service to the downtrodden could be rendered only by working physically at the grass roots'. At this point, he decided to quit his professorial job and work on Asha's educational projects in Uttar Pradesh.

Sandeep's decision was something of a jolt to his father, who had earlier dreamt of his son becoming a civil servant. His mother Uma was more supportive in his decision since her own father had been a prominent social worker. Sandeep's wife Arundhati, who had been associated with the Narmada Bachao Andolan, stood by him in his leaving conventional employment for grass-roots work. Soon, his father's innate belief in his son's ability and integrity overcame other fears and he was able to accept this initiative on Sandeep's part.

From the rarefied, pampered campus of a premier institution like IIT, Kanpur, Sandeep headed straight to Ballia in Uttar Pradesh, home to his paternal grandfather's family. Here he encountered the most disturbing social and economic realities of Indian villages—a lack of basic facilities, poor health of the people, cruel discrimination practised against lower castes and Dalits, and the vulnerable position of girl children, considered fit only for household chores by their families, never for education.

Sandeep's initiative in the face of these conditions was to unite with local volunteers and set up an Asha school in the Reoti town of Ballia district in 1994. While this provided primary education up to Class VI, a sewing class for women was set up later that has seen several batches of women learn tailoring. Making the best use of available conditions is a hallmark of Asha projects. One school, currently being attended by girls from the Bhar and fisherfolk community, was set up in a building that used to be a post office, then moved to the premises of a temple on the outskirts of Reoti town. The tailoring class was set up with used sewing machines that had been donated to Asha. Since there is total transparency in the Asha scheme of things, overhead expenses are kept to the barest minimum and no money is spent on gleaming infrastructure.

Livelihood projects that enable people to become self-reliant are a priority with Asha. In Ballia, along with bee-keeping, candles, incense sticks, patchwork bed covers, chalk, handmade greeting cards and chyawanprash, were tried as products. Bee-keeping is done and handmade greeting cards are currently being made by some Asha volunteers who have pooled their resources and taken up cooperative farming. Citronella is being cultivated on these patches of land, and a distillation column to extract aromatic oil from it has also been installed. Activities that encourage self-reliance, the extremely nominal fees collected from Asha students, and a lump sum donated years earlier by an Asha–Berkeley well-wisher that forms a corpus fund, are the sources for Asha's finances in Ballia.

From his work at the grass roots, and by observing the conditions at the many Asha projects in India in UP, Karnataka, Tamil Nadu, Andhra Pradesh, Jharkhand and Assam, Sandeep was able to recognize the problem of education for the rural and disadvantaged population in India. He points out that the Indian education is a legacy of the British, who had put in place a system of schools and colleges to ensure literate clerks and officers for their colonial administration.

Today, when parents send their children to be educated, they are doing it out of a hope that these children will grow up to have secure, low-risk job and a steady income. But the reality is very different from these dreams. After such children have grown to be youths thronging employment exchanges and attending innumerable interviews without success, they have also not learnt any livelihood skills they could have traditionally imbibed from their communities. So farmers, carpenters, bricklayers and craftsmen are all pushed into the schooling machinery and alienated from their traditional occupations. They are rarely ever lucky enough to land the white-collar clerical jobs they have educated themselves to work in. These go to youths from a more privileged background, urban dwellers, with a better grasp of the ruling language, English.

As he saw the effects which large-scale unemployment and the thwarted dreams of millions of people had on the stability of a society, Sandeep realized that a completely different approach to education was needed. He believes, 'Contrary to the popular opinion that education opens up more job opportunities, it rewards only a minuscule percentage of the population, mostly coming from socio-economically privileged groups. It is only the dream of getting these small number of high salaried coveted jobs that has sustained the view that education opens up more job opportunities. If we consider the hard reality, the education system today makes many more people jobless than it is able to provide jobs to. In fact, the process of education is so lopsided and strangulating that it saps the person of all his/her imagination and enthusiasm making him/her unfit for any other work. The state of unemployment in Ballia is such that people holding even Bachelor's and Master's degrees are forced to take up teaching jobs in privately run primary and middle level schools for a meagre Rs 200 to Rs 300 per month. Even a daily wage worker, involved in manual work can earn two or three times more. This crippling effect can only lead to frustration among the people who are unfortunate enough not to secure a job. The government and political parties only make the situation worse by creating an illusion that they can create more jobs. They only fuel the rat race of people going through the education system and then contending for jobs.

'If we are to channelize the energy of our youth for constructive activity in society then we need to work to dispel the notion that education opens up more job opportunities. The sooner we agree to examine the myth that the present education system is a desirable thing, the better it would be for our society. A completely new form of education system with a different purpose altogether, has to be worked out for creating a healthy society' ('More than Schooling: A critique of the modern educational system', Sandeep Pandey, www.indiatogether.com).

In line with this vision, Asha has set up an ashram in Lalpur, a village in Hardoi district, 60 km from Lucknow. Here the model of education is based on a philosophy which works to cultivate values for a just human order, and promotes skills which will help a person become self-reliant. The curriculum is being developed by Asha to help in creating happy and satisfying human relationships. There are abundant opportunities for students to develop creative talents through art and craft activities. Local craft and artisans are well-represented in the learning programme. Health services to the villagers of the area are also a feature of the holistic approach to education that Asha has come to symbolize.

Asha's activities at Lalpur have meant different things to different people. For an elderly Gandhian, Surya Prakash

Srivastava, known locally as 'Babaji', the ashram is the continuation of a dream of social justice and community well-being that he first dreamt in 1932 after encountering Mahatma Gandhi. For Ashok Jain, an aeronautical engineer from IIT, it has meant an opportunity to test ferro-cement construction and alternative building technologies. For the people of Lalpur village, it has meant a social revolution of sorts—a place where all are treated on par, and there is no scope for caste-based differences, or other forms of discrimination. For the vested interests of the area, long used to social practices that gave them an edge over their less fortunate brethren, the ashram is a threat, and they are doing what they can to provide obstacles in its path.

From a vision of three friends that began at Berkeley in 1991, Asha has grown into an organization with thirty-eight chapters in the United States, as well as others in Germany, Switzerland, Holland, the United Kingdom, Australia and Singapore. The overseas chapters raise funds for Asha's activities in India, and have provided a meaningful opportunity for Indians living, studying and working overseas, to help improve the lives of some of the poorest and most deprived people in the country of their birth. What makes it even more special is that this improvement comes in the form of education—the dawning of true wisdom that dispels ignorance and fear, and promotes social equality.

A poignant moment for Asha was the death of one of their founders, V.J.P. Srivatsavoy in 2000. He had been working as an executive with Unilever in Mumbai when he passed away. Deepak Gupta continues to be associated with Asha's activities and teaches at IIT, Kanpur. Sandeep Pandey spends time at

Lucknow, Lalpur, and all the other places where Asha has grass-roots projects going. When he was awarded the Ramon Magsaysay Award for Emergent Leadership in 2002, he initially thought someone was playing a prank on him! This was because at the age of thirty-seven, he was the youngest Indian to have received the award, and in a modest manner he thought that there were many more deserving people engaged in selfless social work in India.

But the award meant recognition not only for his personal attempts, but also for the role that Asha has played as a powerful catalyst for social change in rural India, transcending barriers of caste and gender discrimination.

Sandeep's own convictions have led him to take up a strong stand against militarism and communalism. When the nuclear tests were conducted in Pokharan in May 1999, he participated in the Pokharan to Sarnath march along with many other social activists. This group of people, proponents of peace, was registering its protest at the increased 'arming' of India. Communal violence in Gujarat was a source of deep concern to Sandeep Pandey, and he expressed this by marching with friends and co-activists from Chitrakoot to Ayodhya (two sites closely associated with Sri Rama), protesting against the violence and spreading the message of communal harmony. Such public protests have brought Sandeep in the firing line of those people opposed to his views, and his actions have occasionally been the subject of debate and comment.

In recent times, he has worked to promote understanding between India and Pakistan. In 2001, Asha sponsored a visit by ten girls from Islamabad to India. These girls arrived in India by boarding the 'Dosti' bus at Wagah, and were put up with Indian families during the course of their stay. Even though they reached Lucknow close to midnight, they were overwhelmed to find the platform crowded with welcoming children, well-wishers and reporters. Ironically, some reporters began interviewing local Lucknow girls thinking they were from Pakistan! This, more than anything else, underlined that we need to put aside our differences, and increase friendship between the two countries.

As a child of independent India, Sandeep is a fierce campaigner for the creation of a healthy society 'where all the needs of all human beings can be satisfied'. It is natural that for him the idea of education should mean empowerment of the people. That is Asha's greatest achievement—to give the poorest of the poor a reason to hope for a better future.